This engaging book conveys the exci[...] the pleasure of starting your own bus[...] book will drive you on!

Emeritus Professor Ken O'Neill, co-author of *Understanding Enterprise*

The Millennial Millionaire presents keen insights into the lived reality of young entrepreneurs, providing key messages for the next wave of these key economic drivers. The multicultural background of the young entrepreneurs highlighted provides for a unique perspective on being young and in business, and reaffirms the traits that drive entrepreneurial success.

Jonathan Lashley, PhD, Fellow, Sir Arthur Lewis Institute of Social and Economic Studies (SALISES), University of the West Indies, Barbados

Entrepreneurship can be a realistic and tangible goal for so many unemployed young people, helping them to get their lives on track and realise their potential as business owners... We welcome this book on youth entrepreneurship, which will no doubt inspire more budding entrepreneurs to explore, develop and launch their own business ideas.

Martina Milburn, Chief Executive of The Prince's Trust

There has never been a better time to be an entrepreneur, with advancements in technology empowering those with a good idea to thrive. Dhaliwal explores how young people are harnessing this opportunity to create cutting edge, successful businesses that are disrupting the status quo. The inspirational young entrepreneurs featured in this book have all set out to solve the problems they see in the world and are testament to what can be achieved, no matter your age. If you have ever thought about defying convention, throwing caution to the wind and taking the entrepreneurial path, this is the book for you.

Johnny Luk, CEO of NACUE (National Association of College & University Entrepreneurs)

Young people are amongst the most determined and enthusiastic of entrepreneurs and with appropriate advice, often from inspirational and experienced business people, and with skills development, such as can be found in some universities today, they have the potential to be extremely successful.

Professor Sir Christopher M. Snowden, President and Vice-Chancellor, Southampton University, UK

Spinder Dhaliwal's latest book brings together a wide range of fascinating case studies of young entrepreneurs who are responding to emerging opportunities for enterprise. The entrepreneurs' stories underpin the structure of the book by bringing to life chapters ranging from why economies need young entrepreneurs to understanding entrepreneurial teams.

Professor Nigel Lockett FRSA, Professor of Entrepreneurship at Lancaster University Management School, UK

This book explores the rise of 'Millenial Millionaires' – young entrepreneurs who have created new business ideas, implemented them effectively and driven them to succeed and gain the rewards. Millenial Millionaires goes beyond the easy rhetoric and explores the people, the business cases, the context and the approaches which these exceptional entrepreneurs have used to achieve outstanding results. We can all learn and gain inspiration from this book.

Professor David Rae, author of *Opportunity-Centred Entrepreneurship*

The Millennial Millionaire

How young entrepreneurs turn dreams into business

Spinder Dhaliwal

First published 2017 by
PALGRAVE

Palgrave in the UK is an imprint of Macmillan Publishers Limited, registered in England, company number 785998, of 4 Crinan Street, London, N1 9XW.

Palgrave Macmillan in the US is a division of St Martin's Press LLC, 175 Fifth Avenue, New York, NY 10010.

Palgrave is a global imprint of the above companies and is represented throughout the world.

Palgrave® and Macmillan® are registered trademarks in the United States, the United Kingdom, Europe and other countries.

ISBN 978–1–137–56351–4 paperback

This book is printed on paper suitable for recycling and made from fully managed and sustained forest sources. Logging, pulping and manufacturing processes are expected to conform to the environmental regulations of the country of origin.

A catalogue record for this book is available from the British Library.

A catalog record for this book is available from the Library of Congress.

Printed and bound by CPI Group (UK) Ltd, Croydon, CR0 4YY

I dedicate this book to my Mum and Jasmine
for their youthful spirit and to my late father
who made it all possible

Contents

Foreword by Margaret Mountford

Britain used to be described as a nation of shopkeepers. Now, we are a nation of entrepreneurs, the most entrepreneurial country in Europe and fourth in the world, according to the 2015 Global Entrepreneurship Index.

This reflects a sea change in our attitude to starting a business. In the economic doldrums following the global financial crisis in 2008, the government called for an 'enterprise-led recovery', and both the public and the private sector started to take positive steps to encourage the creation of new businesses. StartUp Britain was formed in 2011 to help to galvanise the sector, to offer inspiration, resources and guidance to new and prospective entrepreneurs. The government's Start-Up Loans scheme was launched in 2012, to provide access to funds and mentoring, and thousands of aspiring entrepreneurs have taken advantage of it. And while changes in consumer demands have led to the demise or shrinkage of many of our traditional businesses, technological advances have made it easier than ever before to start others.

Entrepreneurship is now seen as the solution to the UK's economic problems, leading to the creation of employment and the generation of wealth. Young people still at school are encouraged to think of starting their own businesses; enterprise competitions test their ideas and their ability to draw up business plans and to work in teams. There were over 600,000 start-ups in the UK in 2015 alone, and many and varied indeed are the organisations which purport to help young, and not-so-young, people who want to be entrepreneurs.

Are entrepreneurs born and not made? I have always thought that there are qualities which you either have or you don't: determination, drive, resilience, the will to succeed, an acceptance that risks have to be taken and that failure can be a tool for success. But even these innate qualities can be honed and developed by education and experience. Of fundamental importance is an ability to work very, very hard for long periods of time, and then even harder and longer still, but this too can be acquired by practice.

And of course there are lessons to be learned from people who have been there and done it, who have succeeded in creating a successful business, and not necessarily at the first attempt. One of the hardest things in life is to realise what you don't know, and often it is only when you see someone doing what you are trying to do, and succeeding, that you can identify where you are going wrong. We all learn by our mistakes, but it is much better to learn from someone else's mistakes, if they are willing to tell you about them, and advice is much more likely to be accepted if it is backed by practical experience which bears it out.

Everyone starting up a business needs to believe in their product, or service, or brand, and in their own ability to deliver, but not everyone can do that on their own. They need to be inspired, they need the example of others who have created a successful business, and the most effective examples are those of their peers.

Nor should anyone think that a business has to be big in order to be a success. We hear a lot about scalability, but not all businesses have huge growth potential, and there is nothing to be ashamed of in remaining a niche business with a small following if that is what you want. Growth for the sake of it makes no sense at all.

So I was very pleased when Spinder invited me to write a foreword to this book, because it provides young people with answers to many of the issues I have just raised: How can I find out who to go to for help? What sort of education or training do I need? How do I know if my idea a good one? And most importantly, tell me about some people who have succeeded.

Success has not come easily to all the young entrepreneurs featured in this book, but they have all persevered. No one should think that starting a business will be easy. For some, having the idea will be the easy bit, while others will struggle to come up with a viable business idea but once they do, they will forge ahead.

Many new businesses fail, and not every successful business will produce a millionaire, but I hope that this book will provide inspiration to those who are starting out on the entrepreneurship journey, and that the young entrepreneurs featured here will not merely achieve more success in their own businesses but will also encourage many others to follow in their footsteps.

Margaret Mountford
Chairman, Bright Ideas Trust

Foreword by Lord Karan Bilimoria

The millennial generation is the key to transforming our economy worldwide, and entrepreneurship is one route. Today, far more than ever before, entrepreneurship presents young people with opportunities to express their creativity and take their talents and knowledge in new directions. The challenge to develop new technologies and innovations for commercial application has brought out the best in entrepreneurs. In the digital world we see big ideas with huge potential for impact.

For some, be it through background, attitude, education or passion, there is little choice but to carve out your own path. Entrepreneurship remains a great way of lifting people out of poverty or disadvantage and allowing young people to explore new avenues. It brings new opportunities to people of all backgrounds, with any qualification or none. It is crucial that entrepreneurs and experts share what they know and that creativity is nurtured, rather than discouraged. As an Enterprise Leader for The Prince's Trust I have seen many young entrepreneurs gain confidence as they engage with mentors and learn how to run a business effectively.

Starting a business is never easy. It takes guts for a young individual to decide to go it alone, without knowing what lies ahead. New, fast-growing small businesses make up just 1 per cent of all companies registered in the UK, but according to the Centre for Economics and Business Research, they add 4,500 jobs to our economy every week. Our economy relies on their commitment and devotion to their ventures, as well as their blue-sky thinking.

I too, started business as a young graduate and I was in debt. When I first arrived in Britain in the 1980s, all I was taught about entrepreneurship was that it was a dirty word.

When the time came to decide which career path I wanted to take, my family discouraged me from becoming an entrepreneur. When I started my first venture, importing polo sticks from India to sell to large department stores in London, my father, clearly unimpressed, told me, 'Karan, you are wasting your education, becoming an import-export wallah!'

The world is a very different place now; there are now big businesses that foster an entrepreneurial spirit in their workforce, and individual entrepreneurs have worked hard to earn our trust. That is why I welcome this book by Spinder Dhaliwal.

I have known Spinder for many years in a career spanning several universities. She is well known as an academic and writer and compiled the Asian Rich List for several years so she knows all about success. Spinder is well networked and enthusiastic about her subject, and has developed entrepreneurship programmes and modules. More importantly, she really understands the people she writes about and wants to inspire others through her writing.

Across the world, young entrepreneurs will be the next generation's mentors and role models, and if enterprise is more accessible to young people of any background, more people will have the opportunity to forge a career of their choice. Others will learn by example and mentorship, and the benefits will spread.

In my capacity as a university Chancellor I have been an advocate of good entrepreneurial education. I have watched universities take a greater role in creating the next generation of entrepreneurs and encouraged greater links between education and industry to help self-starters flourish.

This is why the kind of experiences shown in this book are so important. If the path of entrepreneurship is closed to many young people, then many who are deserving and talented will get left behind, and many opportunities will remain unknown to successive generations. The stories told in this book could inspire more people to bring innovations, designs, new technologies and digital services to market, and the value of that is considerable.

Lord Karan Bilimoria CBE DL
Founder and Chair of Cobra Beer

About the Author

Dr Spinder Dhaliwal is the Director of Postgraduate Programmes at the University of Westminster's Business School and a Reader in Entrepreneurship. She was previously at the University of Surrey where she headed the MBA Entrepreneurship module and was Programme leader for MSc Entrepreneurship. Spinder has taken students and aspiring entrepreneurs through Entrepreneurship programmes both in the UK and overseas.

Avoiding the insularity of many in her profession, Spinder's work targets, and hits, a much wider audience than just students and other academics. She has been a regular contributor to the media and, in the past few years, has become an increasingly influential figure in more mainstream circles. Spinder and her work have been profiled in the *Independent*, the *Guardian* and the *Daily Mail* and she has appeared on the BBC's flagship *Breakfast News* programme.

Spinder has developed what the *Daily Mail* described as a 'high flying career' which spans academia, writing and the media. Spinder has written extensively about entrepreneurship and the business community and compiled Britain's Richest Asians, reflecting her long-held interest in the field. Her book *Making a Fortune – Learning from the Asian Phenomenon* (2008) has been noted widely.

Featured Young Entrepreneurs

Georgie Bullen – Team Insight

Visually impaired from a young age, Georgie made her Paralympic debut at London 2012. After the Paralympics Georgie, then 18, decided to combine her passion for Goalball with her determination to educate people in visual impairment awareness, which was how Team Insight was created. Team Insight uses the Paralympic sport of Goalball as a unique team - building experience which not only strengthens communication, trust and teamwork amongst groups, but also dramatically improves their visual impairment awareness.

Solveiga Pakštaitė – Design by Sol

Lithuanian Solveiga is the brains behind Design By Sol, which she started at age 22. Solveiga is a designer who specialises in user-centred and sustainable design and is passionate about creating elegant, intuitive and beautiful products that improve the quality of our everyday lives. She is the inventor of Bump Mark, a bio-reactive expiry label for food that will help dramatically cut food waste by indicating when the food actually goes bad. The product has a patent pending and has been awarded prizes, various grants and has gained huge amounts of publicity worldwide.

Sarah Watkinson – Yull Shoes

Shoe expert Sarah is the creative director of Yull Shoes. At 18, Sarah completed a foundation course in fashion at the London College of Fashion before going to the University of Westminster where she studied as an undergraduate in Business Management, majoring in entrepreneurship. Her business and education journey went hand in hand as she started getting her shoes manufactured in China just as her degree began. Her hard work and desire to be a top British brand means she is forging a name for herself.

Kristian Else – Hallbookers.co.uk

The young Australian, then 21, who studied at the University of Westminster, said the poor condition of his halls seriously affected his university experience, grades and even well-being. But rather than ignoring the issue, he decided to fight back and launched review website Hallbookers.co.uk to prevent others going through tough times.

Nigel Westwood – Avelere

Nigel Westwood, co-founder of Avelere, studied with Norwegian Guno Stuan before forming a business together straight after university. The Scandinavian influence plays a huge role in the style of Avelere where they design and manufacture furniture and homewares. They put an interesting twist on furniture products and Nigel deals with outsourcing their manufacturing. They tried a few other businesses before Avelere, including handbag inserts which Nigel, then 22, made himself and which helped finance Avelere.

Mathew Simmonds – SpeakSet

Oxford-educated Matt Simmonds, then 23, is the co-founder of SpeakSet. Together with Adi Kasliwal and Ewan Marshall they have transformed the way older people connect with technology. Tackling the issue of isolation head on, they have eased the fears of the elderly with their high-tech solutions. These young entrepreneurs are helping the elderly with an age - defying video calling system that connects them to the world. Matt also boasts having designed components for the McLaren Formula One car.

Demi Owoseje – Majeurs Chesterfield

Demi Owoseje from East London set up Majeurs Chesterfield, when she was 24 years old. The company sources and restores old leather furniture to sell back to the public through the company's website. Demi also offers a service which up-cycles and restores pieces that belong to the public. She works out of a workshop and showroom in Surrey Quays in South East London.

Gaby Evans – Gabrielle Gardens

Gaby Evans, from Hackney, has secured a Gold medal at the world-class RHS Hampton Court Palace Flower Show, after receiving help setting up in business from youth charity, The Prince's Trust. Gaby was made redundant following the UK recession. She struggled for a year to find a steady job, which led her to feeling anxious and depressed about her future. After successfully completing the Prince's Trust programme, Gaby, then 28, set up a garden maintenance company – called Gabrielle Gardens – and as her reputation grew, so did her client base.

Amit Pate – Snaptivity

Indian-born entrepreneur Amit Pate encapsulates the dreams of many international students. Amit came to the UK to study for a Masters degree at the age of 24 and, together with a friend, won a start-up competition for their business idea of anti-counterfeiting technology. Persistence and perseverance paid off as he later won a coveted place on the UK Sirius programme, beating off tough worldwide competition. He is now the entrepreneur behind Snaptivity, which enables you to find yourself in photos no matter who takes them, along with two other co-founders, Phong Vu and Volha Paulovich.

Charlie Davies – iGeolise

Charlie graduated from Cardiff University in 2008 and co-founded iGeolise in 2009 with his business partner, Peter Lilley. Their high tech company focuses on the time it takes to reach a location rather than the distance.

Charlie, who started the business at 26, is a great communicator and has the rare gift of translating geek-speak into plain English. He's an intuitive problem solver. Always has been, always will be – he simply likes knowing how and why things work. And also why they don't and how to fix them. Charlie is an astute marketer with a great business brain whose contribution to iGeolise goes way beyond the technology.

Conno Christou – Avocarrot

Greek-Cypriot Conno Christou, began his business career at 24 and boasts the kind of life many high-tech wannabes only dream of. His eventful business life has taken him from Cyprus to London to the US Silicon Valley and Athens. He is part of a strong team, with George Eracleous, George Makkoulis and Panos Papageorgiou, initiated by the four friends and culminating in their company Avocarrot, a network site for native advertising. Avocarrot has also been recognised as 1 of the 8 best companies from Google for Entrepreneurs in a global competition and voted as the 'Next Big Thing' at the advertising technology conference ad:tech in 2013.

Corey Anderson Boyce – Supreme Delights

Barbados-born and bred Corey Anderson Boyce is a man with a mission. He wants to be employed and to provide employment to as many others as he can. Frustrated with being out of work or in low-paid seasonal work, Corey, at the age of 25, decided to take his destiny in his own hands and create a confectionary business from the best the island has to offer. Sweet-toothed Corey is the owner of the fledgling company Supreme Delights, bringing traditional confectionaries with an added twist of different flavours to the market.

Acknowledgements

Having taken hundreds of students through entrepreneurship programmes in my capacity as an academic, I have been impressed with their energy, passion and drive. Be they undergraduate, postgraduate, MBA or executive students, they came up with some creative business ideas.

I was fortunate enough to travel the world delivering courses in entrepreneurship to students in Barbados, Mauritius, Greece, Hong Kong, Singapore and China. Apart from being amazing places to visit, in each country each cohort of students was different. I experienced diverse cultures, different teaching and learning styles, varying aspirations and uncertain job prospects. However, what was the same was their level of creativity and enthusiasm and it was a real privilege to see the students blossom because they were given the opportunity to come up with a business idea and to pitch it to an audience in a safe environment. Hopefully, each student grew from the experience.

Many have gone on to run successful businesses; others have joined family firms and used their newfound knowledge to take them forward. Still others opted for corporate life and use their skills to help established enterprises, while others still hanker for their dreams.

Today, we face a challenging world – the issues are real and the young entrepreneurs featured in this book are real. Working with young fledgling entrepreneurs with so much potential, enthusiasm and energy directed into creative, innovative ideas has been inspirational. If I can motivate some more, then my work is done.

I am grateful to The Prince's Trust, Shell LiveWIRE, Matt Clifford, Harry Shepherd, Jonathan Lashley, Jane Chang and Agata Mazurkiewicz for introducing me to the young entrepreneurs featured in this book and I thank Paul Tosey, Bal Basra, Jasmine Basra, Jenny Hindley, Andrew Malvern and Ursula Gavin for their support and, of course, a special thanks to all the young entrepreneurs.

Spinder Dhaliwal

Young Entrepreneurs – Why Do We Need Them?

Imagine having a £1 million turnover while you're still under 30. The people featured in this book didn't just imagine it; they're working towards it. Through entrepreneurial skill, astounding levels of self-motivation and creativity, they are making the grade. Some of their businesses are traditional, some online and some downright quirky. All of their stories are compelling and inspirational.

This book features young guns that illustrate the entrepreneurial success story. It charts their journey, showing how they started, who inspired them, how they financed their business and, above all, what young wannabes can learn from their stories.

Now, more than ever before, young people want to make it big and this book is clearly and unashamedly aimed at them. Furthermore, it is not based on speculation but is an analysis of real success. It describes examples that really happened and shows you how you can achieve success too.

This book enables you to share the experience of the highs and lows of being young and in business. It will help you understand the barriers and challenges of starting and running a business and how they can be overcome. This book will help you see how others overcame hurdles to create successful businesses. It offers good advice from young entrepreneurs who have successfully started 'living the dream' to help motivate and inspire you.

So, why do we need young entrepreneurs?

In today's world of change and uncertainty we need the talents of entrepreneurs more than ever, according to Thompson (2004). Throughout this book, we see examples of what Thompson called *the facets of an entrepreneur.* These include focus, advantage, creativity, ego, team and social dimensions. The facets framework can provide insights to help entrepreneurs and would-be entrepreneurs understand their strengths and potential, and identify those areas requiring support. The entrepreneurs featured in this book have been open to opportunities, found gaps in the market and used their grit and determination to go forward.

At the cutting edge of the entrepreneurial community are young entrepreneurs. Young entrepreneurs are needed to rescue and revitalise the economy, according to Lord Alan Sugar in his search for his *Junior Apprentice*. Arjun Rajyagor, the bespectacled 17-year-old winner of the first series, did not obviously replicate Sugar's killer instinct. However, the inexperience of youth could be just the tonic the economy needs. Young entrepreneurs with their energy, drive, confidence and resilience could yet be the perfect formula for entrepreneurial success.

Reality business shows such as *The Apprentice, Million Dollar Intern* and the established *Dragon's Den* serve to popularise the spirit of entrepreneurship. According to Nigel Lockett, Professor of Entrepreneurship at Lancaster Management School, this high media presence means, 'it has never been easier to be an entrepreneur'.

The skills young people have today are vital too. Lockett explains, 'Young entrepreneurs are more familiar with today's technology which is driving enterprise and has spawned so many opportunities, not just for internet businesses, but also in supporting traditional businesses.' This generation has grown up with the Internet, smartphones and the instantaneous nature of social networking sites. 'They are finding ways to work smarter not harder. They are fiercely ambitious and do not want to waste time.'

So, does business hold more interest than studying? Many of our most renowned entrepreneurs left school as early as they could – Richard Branson, Alan Sugar and hotelier Surinder Arora are a few of many who learnt by doing. However, despite these role models, it appears that many young people are finding their entrepreneurial wings whilst studying. Sarah Yull illustrates this in Chapter 5.

Let's see what inspires young people to become entrepreneurs. Edwin Broni-Mensah launched his Internet business www.givemetap.com whilst completing his PhD in mathematics at the University of Manchester. Edwin was set on entering investment banking until he was approached by a friend to join as a director in a start-up company. 'This taste of entrepreneurship was enough for me to know that entrepreneurship was fascinating, challenging and above all so much fun!' Edwin recalls. He hasn't looked back since. His enterprise enables users of specially branded stainless steel bottles to obtain free refills of tap water from a network of cafés and restaurants across major cities. For every GiveMeTap bottle sold they provide a person in Africa with clean drinking water for five years through the development of water boreholes.

Hermione Way started her business www.newspepper.com at the age of 22. Family influences were key: 'My older brother had his own business, so I am very lucky to have been exposed to the entrepreneurial mind set at a young age.' So too was her natural curiosity and impatience: 'Most of my business ideas come from me wanting to solve problems that I encounter in my daily life and thinking "Why aren't they doing it like that?"'

Hermione started her first venture, newspepper.com, during her second year of university: 'The idea was born out of anger and frustration over what my university were teaching me at a time when I was witnessing my industry rapidly changing.' She recalls, 'I was doing a degree in Journalism and was only being taught newspaper journalism, at a time when newspapers were in decline and print was going digital. By the time I graduated my company was earning enough revenue for me to run it full time!'

The type of people you meet is rewarding too. Comparing herself to her employed peers, Hermione observes, 'When you are the founder of a small company or start-up you meet people in larger companies at a much higher level than you would normally meet if you just worked for a company.' This level of networking is a confidence booster.

It's not all play, though. 'It takes lots of energy! You have to put your time and energy into it twenty-four-seven to make it prosper and grow, it's demanding and challenging, but well worth it!' says Hermione.

For Hermione, the advantages of being young and in business are that you can spot opportunities in the market for innovation where others may have become stagnant or too big to be innovative. You can also spot where new technologies can enable you to offer products and services more easily and more cheaply than competitors. It's fantastic too if you decide to go into corporate life later.

Another young entrepreneur, Oxford graduate Rajeeb Dey (CEO of Enternships.com), has several businesses and stumbled into entrepreneurship by accident. 'I was 17 years old and decided to start an organisation that would work to give school students a voice in their education.' He launched the English Secondary Students' Association (ESSA) and set up www.studentvoice.co.uk. 'Having established ESSA I realised how fun and fulfilling it is to see an idea come into fruition.' ESSA is the first student-run organisation that gives a voice to secondary school children. Today, ESSA works with thousands of students across England.

Rajeeb stresses the importance of networking: 'I meet a whole array of interesting and inspiring people – networking is an essential part of being an entrepreneur and something I really enjoy!' However, the start-up process can be challenging and many resort to 'bootstrapping' which is the minimal use of financial resources. 'When you are just starting and "bootstrapping" your business with little/no resources you have to fulfil numerous functions all at once as you do not have the luxury of hiring a big team to support you.'

Rajeeb concedes there are numerous advantages to being young and in business. 'Firstly you'll be surprised by how many more experienced and older people there are in business willing to help you and support you in your journey; secondly as you're young you have fewer commitments, you're unlikely to have a family to support and thus can take more risk. Finally the, often naïve, optimism always helps as you're less likely to have become jaded by any previous negative experiences!'

Setting the context

'The real measure of success comes, not during times of comfort and convenience, but at times of challenge and controversy,' wrote Martin Luther King. The world has indeed become more challenging and also more controversial. In a decade when the economy has teetered on the brink of recession, propped up by short-term consumer spending and rising house prices, where stock market values, not only in the UK but at a global level, have fluctuated sharply and where faith and trust in institutions and role models have been significantly diminished, this book offers what Gandhi referred to as 'optimism on solid facts'.

It's interesting to note the international picture when it comes to young entrepreneurs. The world will need around half a billion jobs by 2030, according to Andrew Davenport, CEO of Youth Business International (2013), as more and more young people join the labour market.

This is an alarming statistic given the current weak economic growth and recovery together with escalating youth unemployment and underemployment rates. Companies cannot provide all these jobs and so encouraging enterprise for the young is key. After all, young people in business are the phenomenon that will change the future landscape; they will offer hope in a turbulent world. Entrepreneurs create wealth and jobs.

The Global Enterprise Monitor (GEM) defines entrepreneurship as 'any attempt at new business or new venture creation, such as self-employment, a new organisation, or the expansion of an existing business by an individual, a team of individuals, or an established business'. A joint report by the GEM and Youth Business International (YBI) in 2013 found that young people up to the age of 35 are the most likely to start a business. Thus efforts must be made to support them (Kew *et al.*, 2013). Encouraging young entrepreneurs is not just an aspiration. It is a necessity.

The benefits are considerable, as young entrepreneurs are likely to create jobs that employ other young people. They are more responsive to new economic opportunities and trends and are more innovative. Young people with entrepreneurial skills also make better employees. An employable graduate might not be enterprising, but an enterprising graduate will be employable.

The role of entrepreneurial education together with entrepreneurial experience can help young people develop new skills that can be applied to other challenges in life. Entrepreneurial skills such as opportunity recognition, innovation, critical thinking, resilience, decision-making, teamwork and leadership will benefit the young whether or not they intend to continue as entrepreneurs.

Today, over 73 million people are estimated to be unemployed globally (report by GEM and YBI, 2013). According to the International Labour Office (ILO) young people are three times more likely than adults to be unemployed. The figures will continue to rise unless alternative employment options are encouraged. There is no longer the safety of a job-for-life career path. In Europe, for example, an increasing proportion of young people are involved in temporary employment and part-time work (Erasmus report, 2014).

Entrepreneurship is the way forward in promoting job creation. It is widely recognised that we must nurture the next generation of business leaders who have the advantage of energy and drive and are able to tap into new technology and smart businesses with ease, as well as having a social conscience. More must be done to encourage and support these young entrepreneurs. Families, the education system, big business and the government all have an important role to play.

Enterprise education is crucial, and schools, colleges and universities need to consider the range of skills to instil in the business leaders of tomorrow. Young people need to be creative, innovative, tech-savvy, have a social conscience and need to challenge the status quo, as well as embracing failure and learning and growing from it.

Being a student today is financially tougher than it has ever been. Many students leave university carrying the burden of enormous debt. They are reluctant to borrow more money on risky ideas. The education system must equip young people with skills such as critical thinking, emotional intelligence and problem-solving to give them the confidence to succeed as an entrepreneur. They should have access to entrepreneurial role models who inspire and motivate them and allow them to learn from the successes and failures of others.

Universities around the world are recognising the importance of entrepreneurship as the future of management education. Most universities offer entrepreneurship degrees and modules. Entrepreneurship programmes enable students to simulate the behaviours of entrepreneurs through reflecting on themselves and tapping into their entrepreneurial capabilities. Whether they want to start their own business, add value to a large organisation or anything else, these programmes prepare them to face these challenges. They have the opportunity to be dynamic and creative.

The chapters in this book and the profiles of the entrepreneurs are self-standing and are there to inspire, to motivate and learn from.

This book looks at why we need young entrepreneurs. It looks at their mindset and personality and how they create and spot opportunities. Schools, colleges and universities can make a huge difference, and we look at what works best and what more can be done to support young entrepreneurs. There are some great graduate businesses so we follow the entrepreneurs behind these successes.

There is a strong case for governments to be more proactive and to do more in supporting young entrepreneurs who will be the job and wealth creators of the future.

Social media plays an enormous and increasingly important role in business and examples of this are illustrated throughout the book.

Technology plays a pivotal role for young entrepreneurs who have grown up with it. Technical ideas such as virtual businesses, use of online technology and 'smart' businesses are illustrated. In an era of social media, where nothing remains secret, young entrepreneurs have some powerful marketing tools at their disposal at very low cost.

Organisations such as The Prince's Trust, Shell LiveWIRE, Bright Ideas Trust and the Royal Bank of Scotland, for example, do much to promote entrepreneurship and are great for any fledgling entrepreneur. Competitions serve to raise profiles, while awards, prizes and grants are precious seed funding for many new businesses. More than half of young people in the UK indicated that not having enough money is what would prevent them from starting a business. Access to finance remains an issue despite family assistance. Bootstrapping remains the way to go in the early stages for many of our young entrepreneurs.

Accessing funds is a major headache for new entrepreneurs and particularly so for young entrepreneurs who do not have years of savings behind them. In Chapter 8, we look at what support is available and how best to access it. The role of family in terms of support, encouragement and finance is important, and families are often the first source of seed capital. Issues of support, both formal and informal, will be discussed and these will look at the specific barriers facing young entrepreneurs such as resources, capital and experience, and also the benefits and advantages they may have – for example, they can take greater risks, have more energy and are more tech-savvy.

Who is this book for?

This book is for anyone thinking about enterprise. It's useful both for students doing 'practical' enterprise as part of a curriculum and for those who are actually thinking of starting their own business, as well as those who educate, support or mentor young entrepreneurs. This book gives budding entrepreneurs and students a head start into the entrepreneurial world whatever their background and discipline.

Young entrepreneurs may be part of the answer to societal and economic problems and may provide a new generation of socially and environmentally aware businesses as well as being compelling and inspirational role models.

Natural talent and hard work coupled with an ability to perform when pressure is at its highest win gold medals, and what all the people in this book demonstrate are the same qualities. Serious people. Serious times. Serious business. The least we can do is recognise them. Celebrate them? Yes. Let's.

Still want to make that million? Read on to find out more. And don't just read, visit our website to watch videos of some of the young entrepreneurs at www.he.palgrave.com/dhaliwal-millionaire.

References

European Commission (2014). *Statistical Analysis of the Erasmus for Young Entrepreneurs Programme*, European Commission, Directorate-General for Enterprise and Industry.

Kew, J., M. Herrington, Y. Litovsky and H. Gale (2013). *Generation Entrepreneur? The state of global youth entrepreneurship*. Joint Report: Global Enterprise Monitor (GEM) and Youth Business International (YBI).

Thompson, J. (2004). 'The FACETS of the entrepreneur: identifying entrepreneurial potential', *Management Decision*, 42(2), pp. 243–58.

2 Fast Fortunes – Global Examples of Early Success

Fast and furious, that's the pace of enterprise for the younger generation today. We are now seeing more and more young entrepreneurs appear in global rich lists, and it's worth noting the pace and direction of this movement and what sectors they are in. Businesses owned by young entrepreneurs are diverse and include traditional businesses such as property and fashion as well as high-tech businesses such as apps and specialist websites. They're young and they're rich – young entrepreneurs are set to be the new 'captains of industry'.

If you have a Facebook account or have used Snapchat and Uber then you have helped make billionaires of some very young entrepreneurs. The wealthiest and best known is Mark Zuckerberg, CEO and co-founder of Facebook, the online social networking service. From his dormitory room as a Harvard student, together with four other students, he launched Facebook. In 2007, at the age of 23, Zuckerberg became a billionaire due to the enormous global success of Facebook. More importantly, Facebook has become so ingrained in the global culture, with over 1.44 billion users, it is a phenomenon that has shrunk the planet.

The technology era has opened doors for budding entrepreneurs and enabled them to start up businesses cheaply and quickly. You can start a business in less than 20 minutes online and some of these have grown to see enormous success and have made fortunes for their owners. By the time he was 25, tech-savvy billionaire Evan Spiegel had become one of America's most successful Internet entrepreneurs with his Snapchat app. The app is ethically sound and has captured the way photographs have changed. We used to take photographs of important memories and major events but today pictures are being used for talking. Smartphones and other devices make this so easy. People talk and send photos on Snapchat daily.

The big question is, are entrepreneurs born or bred? One would expect you to be more entrepreneurial if you grew up in a family of entrepreneurs.

This is not always the case. Evan was not born into a family of entrepreneurs; his parents were lawyers and he grew up in Los Angeles and later went to Stanford University. He proposed Snapchat in a class project while at Stanford and even left university to focus on it before completing his degree. Spiegel designed the Snapchat logo in his bedroom. The distinctive yellow-colour social app attracts 200 million daily users and allows them to send and receive pictures and messages that are instantly deleted. Persistence is an important quality for an entrepreneur; Snapchat was not an instant hit, and six months after its launch no one was using it. Spiegel persevered and his company now employs 450 people who work innovatively in a playful environment that stimulates creativity. The app is aimed at 13–25-year-olds and socially conscious Spiegel even released a video to parents explaining Snapchat, thus ensuring a responsible approach to the business. It paid off.

Creativity and innovation play an important role in entrepreneurship. You need to be open to opportunities and also able to create them (Bolton and Thompson, 2002; Rae, 2014). Inspiration can come from observing what's around you, but you need to be alert to opportunities. An example of a lesser known but rising star is Brian Wong who founded Kiip at the age of 19, a mobile rewards network that has changed the face of mobile advertising. He came across his brainwave when he was on a flight. As he watched people play games on their iPads it occurred to him that advertisers could engage the player much more at key moments by building a targeted reward programme when players were most engaged. He wanted to exploit the game explosion and the adrenalin rush players have. He has gone on to receive over $15 million dollars of funding and Kiip was listed as one of the world's most innovative companies.

Most technology entrepreneurs dream of a giant company paying them a fortune for their product. Nick D'Aloisio, an Australian born, London-bred dynamo, became one of Britain's richest millionaires after selling his Summly app to Yahoo for a reported £15 million. D'Aloisio was just 15 when the app was designed to condense online content into just a few words. The new Internet era has opened many doors and allowed a lot of progress to be made but it has also created demand for instant gratification. We all want everything now, we want it quickly and in a format that allows us to waste no time. Time has become a precious asset in this new age where instant gratification is the norm, not the exception. D'Aloisio was ahead of the pack in creating Summly, which allows news stories to be summed up so readers can quickly get up to speed on all the popular stories and news. It mitigates the need to read through thousands of words. D'Aloisio understood this.

The world is full of success stories. Other examples of young entrepreneurs who spotted opportunities and made them happen are teenager Adam Hildreth, who was only 14 when he got together with his friends to launch the social network 'Dubit', which became one of the biggest teen sites in the UK, giving him millionaire status. American Juliette Brindak launched the website Miss O and Friends at the age of ten. The site is aimed at teenage girls and has the latest celebrity gossip, games, quizzes and feature articles. Juliette went on to launch a line of *Miss O and Friends* books. Self-made millionaire Londoner Jamal Edwards started his own film company at the age of 16 and now owns SBTV, which has a global reach and over 30 million hits on YouTube. Each of these businesses has a clear target market and stemmed from the entrepreneurs' personal interests.

The global economy has provided these high-tech young entrepreneurs with new, strategic and creative ways to get ahead. Dinesh Dhamija, *ebookers.com* founder, once told me, 'the internet works best for pornography, travel and gambling' (Dhaliwal, 2008). He should know; he created an enormously successful global brand and survived the dot-com bubble and beyond while others failed.

Does success generate further success? Some communities are well known for being entrepreneurial. I compiled *Britain's Richest Asians* for a period of six years, and I interviewed many rich, successful entrepreneurs originally from India, Pakistan and East Africa who had made their fortunes in Britain. I went on to write a book, *Making a Fortune, Learning from the Asian Phenomenon* (Dhaliwal, 2008), which charted the phenomenal success of many of these immigrants. Most of them are multimillionaires boasting global companies in sectors as diverse as pharmaceuticals, steel, food production, hotels and fashion. They made their fortunes through grit, determination and hard work. All of them were immigrants, and so had to grasp opportunities in their adoptive country.

Will the new generation of Asian entrepreneurs continue this success story? Do they have the drive their parents had, or have education and a comfortable lifestyle hindered repeating the entrepreneurial success story? They may be too quick to purchase their first Mercedes but, I suspect, they still have much to offer.

Serial entrepreneur Gurbaksh Chahal has created, built and grown two businesses by the age of 30. He sold his ad network BlueLithium to Yahoo for an estimated $300 million in 2007, and at that time it was the fifth largest ad network in the US and the second largest in the UK. His success continues as the CEO of gWallet, which is an online monetisation platform offering social gaming developers a variety of ways to monetise their apps. Publicity shy but worth an estimated $80 million and growing is Naveen Selvadurai, co-founder of Foursquare. Foursquare is a local search and discovery app which takes into account the places a user goes to and what they like, and provides recommendations in their current location. Enormously successful, with around 45 million users worldwide and over 200 employees, it has made Naveen his fortune.

American Asian Farrhad Acidwalla, 22, made his fortune as the founder of Rockstah, a web development and media company. From a modest start of $10 seed funding borrowed from his parents he purchased his domain name and came up with a slogan 'creating awesomeness'. He built up the business and then sold it, making him a millionaire. Meanwhile, a more studious Anshul Samar at the age of 13 was determined to make chemistry fun, and his Alchemist Empire creates characters in a fantasy-style game. Young people want to work smart rather than work hard and this is a global phenomenon.

Japan boasts one of Asia's youngest billionaires. Yoshikazu Tanaka founded mobile social gaming Gree, at the age of 26, which is now valued at over £2 billion. China too has its share of burgeoning young entrepreneurs. Forbes China has a list bragging of players such as 29-year-old Chen Di, CEO of Youmi, entertainments; and Mingo Chin, also 29 and CEO of Internet company Wei Wo.

Whilst Internet businesses do seem to make the big bucks, some young entrepreneurs focus on products and services. African Christian Ngan left France after working in the financial services industry and returned home to Cameroon with a reported $3,000 of savings. He founded Madlyn Cazalis, a handmade bio cosmetic company producing body oils, natural lotions and creams and now sells to retail outlets across Cameroon and Central Africa. Ethiopian entrepreneur Senai Wolderufael is the founder of Feed Green Ethiopia Exports company, which produces popular Ethiopian spice blends such as Shiro, Mitmita and Berbere to a primarily Ethiopia diaspora in the US and Europe. This new company only employs women. Young entrepreneurs have a heart, a social conscience and are ready to change the world.

In the Caribbean, Barbados-born Corey Anderson Boyce, the young owner of new company Supreme Delights, has started a business from home utilising local produce such as yams and cassava to make traditional Bajan confectionery. He was fed up with sporadic offers of work and decided to take matters into his own hands. He wants to alleviate unemployment on the island as well as introduce traditional food to a new generation (Cumberbatch, 2014).

Fashion is always at the forefront of a teenager's mind and Madison Robinson, then 15, took this to another level by creating Fish Flops, flip flops with fish designs, and she has now diversified her range of products to t-shirts, hats and apps. From fashion to media, young publishing magnate Savannah Britt, then 14, launched fashion title Girlpez, and boasted the title of being one of the world's youngest publishers.

Irish high-flyer Gary Martin from Londonderry started running his own nightclub at the age of 15, when he was underage to even be there after 9pm. Later, while still at school, he made inroads into the property business which was to make him a wealthy man. After placing an advert in a local paper where he listed his name as 'Gary buys houses' he was inundated with responses. He had built the company into a multimillion empire by the age of 18. Scottish-born millionaire Fraser Doherty was taught how to make jam by his grandmother at the tender age of 14. The boy from Edinburgh went on to leave school at 16 to focus on his 'Super Jam' label and was soon supplying Waitrose nationwide.

Other interesting entrepreneurs include Tim Chae, who boasts two businesses while still a teenager. He dropped out of college to launch social media marketing agency PostRocket. Success has its problems and he was asked to get his father to sign a lease on his apartment. Undeterred, he now encourages other start-ups. Hong Kong magnate Stanley Tang reacted with entrepreneurial flair when his school banned snacks. In true fashion, he spotted an opportunity and brought his own snacks in and sold them to his classmates, thus earning a respectable profit. He went on to become one of the youngest bestsellers at the age of 14 when his book *eMillions* topped the charts.

Innovative British teenager Laurence Rook is turning his fear into a huge success. He was scared of burglars and turned his angst to devising Smart Bell, a special doorbell that deters thieves. When they ring your doorbell, your mobile is immediately notified, and allows you to speak to the visitor.

In the US, children as young as five years are taught the basics of a business during 'lemonade day'. The task is to sell lemonade so if there is a school fete or occasion the children will make lemonade and sell it. One-third of the profits are reinvested into the business to buy ingredients, while one-third are saved and one-third are given to charity. This keeps the spirit of enterprise alive but also teaches essential successful life skills.

All the entrepreneurs discussed in this chapter have had a lot of media exposure but, closer to home, my niece, 10-year-old Jasmine, surprised me by starting her own pretend business organising clutter. Nothing is off limits. This 'business' was initiated by her after being told to tidy her room. Jasmine took to the task with energy and enthusiasm; she researched her business by watching YouTube videos of experts giving tips on cleaning, folding clothes the right way, organising wardrobes and drawers and she immersed herself in the business. She even gave me one of her business cards – literally cut out wonkily from an old tissue box and written by hand. She had a flowery notebook for her customer testimonials – amazing as she didn't actually have any customers. At the age of 10 Jasmine took control of a problem and turned it into a business opportunity, self-driven and totally motivated by her own idea. I see a rosy future ahead of her or at least a tidy bedroom. She illustrates that you're never too young to be an entrepreneur! So let's look at what it takes to be one.

References

Bolton W. K. and J. L. Thomson (2002). *Entrepreneurs: Talent, Temperament, Technique*. Butterworth Heinemann.

Cumberbatch, Shawn (2014). 'Snackers' delight', *Nation News*, 13 July, http://www.nationnews.com/nationnews/news/55417/snackers-delight#sthash.tu3VyG8E.dpuf, date accessed 4 November 2015.

Dhaliwal, S. (2008). *Making a fortune: learning from the Asian phenomenon*. Capstone.

Rae, D. (2014). *Opportunity Centred Entrepreneurship*. Palgrave MacMillan.

Resources

Forbes – www.forbes.com
Startups – www.startups.co.uk/youngentrepreneurs

3 Entrepreneurial Mindset and Personality – What Do You Need to Succeed?

There are enormous advantages to being a young entrepreneur: you have greater energy and motivation and you have less to lose. You do not have to make the decision to leave a highly paid, safe professional job or to start a new venture with a mortgage or children to look after (in most cases). However, while you have more energy and creativity, unfortunately you lack experience; you may be less money savvy; and you don't always know your own strengths and weaknesses so you may be overconfident. Liz Kammel (2012) points out that young entrepreneurs have the advantage of already being fairly poor, with high energy and motivation and no fear about challenging the 'status quo', but they lack experience.

Today we live in a world full of turbulence, change and uncertainty. The choices facing young people today are difficult. Should they study further? What job should they go for? Will they be in debt forever? Choosing to run a business was never a choice in the past. We were expected to take on a trade or profession and have it as a job for life. Career advisors and academics were keen on a risk-averse approach.

Life isn't that simple any more. Being young is harder in terms of the choices that have to be made and the implications of those choices, particularly starting a business. Do you have what it takes? Is it a life-changing experience that makes you? When is the right time to start a business? Can entrepreneurship and education go hand in hand?

So, how can you tell if you've got what it takes?

Bolton and Thompson (2002) define an entrepreneur as 'a person who habitually creates and innovates to build something of recognized value around perceived opportunities'. This could be a team but with an entrepreneurial champion at the core. Thurik (2009) asserts that an entrepreneur is one who takes risks despite uncertainty, who identifies business opportunities and who has the power and resources to exploit those opportunities.

Although these definitions of entrepreneurship differ, the chief key drivers of entrepreneurial activities are efficient use of scarce resources, risk-taking propensity, and sensing opportunities and innovative activities. Debate continues on whether you can actually teach someone to be entrepreneurial or whether he or she is born into the role. If they can be taught, then what skills do they need?

Characteristics such as courage, creativity, curiosity, determination, discipline, empathy, enthusiasm, flexibility, honesty, patience and responsibility are associated with good entrepreneurs (Mariotti, 2014). So are optimism, chance and opportunity. Being a risk-taker, leader and negotiator and possessing self-efficacy (a person's belief about their ability) feature heavily in the entrepreneurship literature (Kirby, 2003; Deakins and Freel, 2012).

Southon and West (2002) take this further and claim that entrepreneurs are confident, charismatic and ambitious, and are impatient, in a hurry and obsessed with work. Interestingly, they are also manipulative in that they use people. Southon and West qualify this in that entrepreneurs may inspire people, pay them and even enable them to achieve things that otherwise they would never be able to on their own.

Entrepreneurship is such a popular buzzword at the moment and television programmes such as *Dragon's Den* and *The Apprentice* highlight this increasingly appealing career path. More recently the *Millionaire Intern* featured successful young entrepreneurs who turned around ailing businesses. The young entrepreneurs who featured in the programme looked at the businesses with fresh eyes, and they had smart ways of improving the businesses whether it was through something as simple as a different layout for the products or by using social media to attract customers and loyalty. It demonstrated a new way of thinking and doing business compared to some tired methods where you display goods in the hope of someone buying them. Now you have to create demand, think of marketing by using social media and offer an efficient service. These days, customers don't want to wait weeks for a delivery – they want it now!

What drives young entrepreneurs?

Entrepreneurs are strongly motivated to overcome obstacles and to achieve (D.C. McClelland, 1961, cited in Kirby, 2003); they feel a great sense of personal control over outcomes (J. B. Rotter, 1966, cited in Kirby, 2003) and the need to manage risk (F. H. Knight, 1921, cited in Kirby, 2003) due to the uncertain nature in which entrepreneurial activity is engaged. Optimism and chance play a role and Chell (2008) discusses the need for achievement, locus of control (the extent to which individuals believe they can control events affecting them) and risk-taking propensity (the degree to which you are prepared to take risks). Storey (2011) combines the role of chance with optimism of the business owner into optimism and chance theory. They need to be open to experience, agreeable and conscientious.

Risk looms large and there is a perception in popular media that entrepreneurs are high risk-takers. In reality, they are moderate risk-takers or calculated risk-takers. They gather information and then make a judgment and only act when they perceive a favourable outcome. What is unique is that they view risk as a challenge in many cases and a situation that may deter others is seen as a possibility for them and they act on the opportunities they spot. According to Timmons (1997), entrepreneurship is an ability to create and build something from practically nothing. It is the act of initiating, doing, achieving and building an enterprise or organisation, rather than simply passively watching, analysing or describing one. It is a knack of sensing an opportunity where others see chaos, contradiction and confusion. A successful entrepreneur is one who takes control and minimises risk either by limiting their financial stake or by reducing the degree of uncertainty, thus making more reliable decisions.

There are many risks facing young entrepreneurs: they are unlikely to have personal savings and may rely heavily on the bank of mum and dad and grandparents.

Young entrepreneurs have to work really hard as it is unlikely that they have people to work for them so they cannot delegate. It's vital for them to build networks and understand and use new technologies. In most cases, like many small business owners, they need to multitask as manager, salesperson, negotiator and so on.

Young entrepreneurs today are lucky in that they grew up with new technologies and social media. This will benefit their businesses and is central to a lot of them. They have grown up in the web era and it is second nature to them.

What young entrepreneurs need is a mindset of faith and belief. They have to make things happen, not wait for them. They must create opportunities, not wait for opportunity to open up for them.

The following example illustrates much of what we have discussed.

Georgie Bullen – Team Insight

Plucked from obscurity at the age of 18 to become a sporting heroine, Paralympian Georgie Bullen is the Director of Team Insight. Visually impaired from an early age, Georgie had the grit and determination to become the youngest player in the UK Goalball team leading to victory at the European Championships in 2009 and then going on to compete in the quarter-finals of the 2012 Paralympics. Using her victories to launch her own business, Team Insight offers the Paralympic sport of Goalball as a team-building exercise and boasts UK-wide corporate clients. Shrewd businesswoman, team player and someone who won't take no for an answer, Georgie is well set to be a major player in the future.

Georgie grew up in a loving family with her two brothers. She was playful and like any young child her future was bright. Events were soon to take a very different turn for the young girl. When Georgie was five years old she went to the opticians and, at first, they thought she had a tumour. Her parents were distraught. They found instead it was visual impairment in one eye. The doctors said it would not get any worse or spread to the other eye. It did get worse and it did spread to the other eye.

It was a major setback for a young child but she continued going to a mainstream school and was resolute not to be wrapped up in cotton wool even at that early age. It forced her to be resilient and forged the character that would lend itself for her to do so well in her business in later years.

She was only seven when both eyes became progressively worse, but was too young to really appreciate the consequences. She liked the sweets she was given before her hospital appointments, but it was hard for her parents who understood the toll this was taking and the future repercussions of her disability. Her teenage years were difficult and especially so at 17, when her friends were learning to drive and she knew she never would be able to. Teenage years can be difficult but she was determined not to wallow.

Her visual impairment meant that Georgie had to spread her A-levels over three years instead of two. It was in the midst of studying for her A-levels that her life was to take another turn.

Georgie had never heard of Goalball before, which is a team sport for blind athletes. 'I had always been rubbish at sports', she confesses. While playing hockey she recalls, 'I would charge at the crowd because I couldn't see the ball!' Regardless, she went to a Paralympian talent identification day and, to her surprise, she got a call back after the event. 'I thought I had got through to the next round', she recalls. But no, she had a big shock upon learning that they wanted her to play for the country and start training with adults. What was more terrifying for her was to play with a blindfold on, thus losing what little sight she had left. It was a rough and ready sport, and she ended up hurt, bruised and battered but euphoric. 'I was thrown in the deep end; I could either sink or swim'. She had assumed that sports for athletes with a visual impairment would be slow and boring so she was shocked at the speed and intensity of the game. At the 2009 European Championships, Georgie made her debut as the youngest player in the Great Britain Women's team. She scored a goal in her first game and the team went on to win gold.

It was exhilarating and she went from novice to the 2012 Paralympian line-up, securing a place in the quarter-finals. It was a whirlwind time and what's more Georgie played the centre position, which is where the most experienced player leads. She was the youngest centre in the Paralympics. 'It was an amazing experience', she remembers with pride, and it was one that was to stand her in good stead for her business career.

The experience raised her profile; she was a sports celebrity and an inspiring role model. However, reality soon beckoned and she went back to her final year of A-levels. Competing in the Paralympics had changed her life and given her a new level of confidence. Nothing was going to hold her back.

Georgie had always expected to go to university but now things were different. Studying presented a massive strain on her eyes. Georgie had a habit of pushing herself with what little sight she had rather than relying on alternative ways of reading and studying. This was going to present a major problem for her going forward with her education. Georgie thought long and hard about going to university, and she did not want to go just for the sake of it. Having sampled the adrenalin of the Paralympics and getting to the quarter-final, she was convinced that she could take Goalball further. A germ of a business idea was sown.

Georgie was 19 years old when she finished her A-levels and started researching for the business, but she had no real idea how to start. Fortunately, her parents were both entrepreneurs and great role models and they inspired her. Her mother had taken over a small housesitting company, Minders Keepers, and turned it into one of the country's leading housesitting organisations. Her father designed exhibitions.

However, still clueless, Georgie turned to The Prince's Trust. She embarked on their week-long enterprise programme, which gave advice on every area of a business. They had a work booklet to complete and lots of talks from experts. They were guided on how to write a business plan, marketing, finance and so on. 'They made you consider every area', Georgie recalls. 'I really had to think about what I was doing.'

The Prince's Trust also put her in touch with a mentor. Georgie met with her mentor every two weeks and found him incredibly useful – she could bounce ideas off him and he gave her business structure. She recalls, 'The Prince's Trust offered a brilliant support network, they are really useful'. However, Georgie, being cautious, decided not to take up funding from The Prince's trust, but instead opted to use her own savings. 'I did not want to start my business with debt.' Her philosophy is: 'The more you can start business without a debt, the better.' Georgie went on to receive a Shell LiveWIRE grand ideas grant of £1,000 in March 2014, just before the launch of her business.

The role of the business mentor is powerful, and they can be incredibly helpful to new entrepreneurs. Georgie's business mentor, Mike Mander, had contacts within the Royal National Institute for Blind people (RNIB), and Georgie was keen on developing a relationship with them to give her business legitimacy, particularly when approaching corporates. She was also keen to raise awareness of the visually impaired. Two-thirds of the visually impaired are unemployed; she really wanted to improve these statistics.

Georgie had to hold a test event for the RNIB to conduct their checks. Pitching is one of the most important skills for an entrepreneur and Georgie had to pitch her business to the RNIB, as she needed their endorsement. It required a lot of preparation to meet their requirements. This was nerve-wracking for her but she got their approval. They were impressed and allowed her to state 'work in collaboration with RNIB' on her website and her certificates were 'approved by the RNIB'. Thus the business had a mission greater than just teambuilding – it had a social conscience.

It was all coming together; the business had goals and structure and solid endorsements. There was clarity in their purpose, which was two-fold: team-building and raising awareness of visual impairment. Their unique selling point was having Paralympians deliver the programme.

Georgie leads the programme, which she developed herself. She has an 'access to work' assistant who is government-funded, as it is essential for her to have a fully sighted person to help, and there is another Paralympian, Mark Powell, who is a judo champ.

Team Insight are offering an exciting and character-building experience, delivered by Paralympians, that strengthens working relationships, develops communication skills, improves team work and creates a sense of trust among colleagues. By having participants blindfolded, they experience what it is like to be visually impaired and gain a greater understanding of how that affects people's lives.

July 2014 was to see the launch event for the business. True to fashion, it was full of local VIPs, companies and the press. The *Cambridge News* covered the event, and the reporter even joined in with the team events.

The whole experience of launching her business has been a huge learning curve. Family, friends, financiers, trainers, advisors, mentors all can play a pivotal role. Georgie had a mentor who gave good advice and went out of his way to open doors for her. Her family was a huge influence as was The Prince's Trust. Georgie was not afraid to ask for help and advice. Entrepreneurial enablers play a huge role in the success stories of entrepreneurs. Don't be afraid to ask for help.

Georgie's main strength as an entrepreneur is her ability to network and also to realise the value of who she is and what she has achieved. 'Goalball has really given me a lot of confidence.' This confidence has helped her greatly and she continually pushes forward with the business, looking for new opportunities: 'I ask to be the guest speaker at networking events, I want people to know about my business.' She is very persuasive.

Georgie knows that she is the unique selling point for the business; her Paralympian status is a great calling card and generates respect instantly, and signals her winning attitude and resilience of character. It also enables people to trust her. Her motto is 'just do it'. She was disabled, with no degree and very young but that did not deter her.

There are benefits to being young, as Georgie explains: 'I had no fear, no mortgage, no major responsibilities.' Georgie continues: 'You also have more room to make mistakes ... if you don't do it when you are young, you may never do it.' The benefits of any entrepreneurial experience are clear, even if you fail; it's looks great on your CV (curriculum vitae) and you grow in experience and maturity so it is character-building.

By now Georgie had experience with sponsors and senior executives from the largest of companies and her confidence was growing. She saw senior executives go from cynical people who did not want to play Goalball to giggling, light-hearted individuals who really bonded with their teams. Goalball broke all barriers; it got them laughing and trusting each other. Georgie has received positive feedback from her clients, and this has generated repeat business.

At the beginning, business was slow; today, they have one event per month but are aiming for two or three per month as their reputation grows. Many of these are repeat bookings and so they are building up loyalty. The next stage is to hire and train salespeople, but Georgie is cautious about growth.

Georgie's best qualities as an entrepreneur are to think quickly on her feet. 'I have complete confidence in whatever I do. I'm happy to go into meetings with executives, I'm happy to cold call, I can push myself to do anything', she asserts. Companies don't always have budgets for team-building; it's not a priority and so Georgie's strategy is to aim for the top companies only: 'I won't take no for an answer and I am really persistent'.

The business is a challenge and from eliciting interest to getting actual bookings is not easy but Georgie is up to the task. She recalls: 'Once I called someone who had received several cold calls prior to mine, but when I said I was a Paralympian and only 20 years old they listened.' She has turned any perceived disadvantage into an enormous gain.

Her sports training has held her in good stead, and she conducts her business in the same way she trains and competes as an athlete. Hard work, practice, experience and resilience are all essential ingredients for success. She is always looking for ways to move forward – standing still is not an option.

Her impairment has not blunted her ability to use her sharp brain, intellect and business acumen together with her sporting prowess. Georgie Bullen made some tough choices and displayed great business acumen. She has drive, enthusiasm and passion and is ahead of the game.

Summary

Georgie's indefatigable spirit encapsulates the entrepreneurial spirit. Her inner self-belief pushed her forward against the odds. Georgie demonstrates a determination and resilience and a get-up-and-go spirit. There is no one single definition of an entrepreneur – each person will have a combination of traits and characteristics. Georgie is aware that she is the unique selling point in her business and has turned her sports acumen into a business opportunity. Georgie understood that she needed to learn about business before jumping in, and so approached The Prince's Trust, reflected on her business idea and built up a great relationship with her mentor who opened doors for her. Whatever your starting point, look at your strengths and build on them – don't let your fear hold you back. Only then will you be alert to opportunities.

Key learnings

- Believe in yourself
- Minimise your debts and go for grant funding
- Get professional support and a good mentor
- Promote yourself at every opportunity and be pitch perfect
- Surround yourself with champions
- Sell, sell, sell!

References

Bolton W. K. and J. L. Thompson (2002). *Entrepreneurs: talent, temperament, technique.* Butterworth Heinemann.
Chell, E. (2008). *The entrepreneurial personality: a social construction.* Routledge.
Deakins, D. and M. Freel (2012). *Entrepreneurship and small firms.* McGraw Hill.
Jovanovic, B. (1982). 'Selection and the evolution of industry', *Econometrica*, vol. 50, no. 3, pp. 649–70.
Kammel, L. (2012). 'Do older or younger entrepreneurs have the greater advantage?', *Forbes*, 3 September.
Kirby, D. (2003). *Entrepreneurship.* McGraw Hill.
Southon, M. and C. West (2002). *The beermat entrepreneur.* Pearson. Prentice Hall.
Storey, D. (2011). 'Optimism and chance: the elephants in the entrepreneurship room', *International Journal of Small Business* vol. 29, no. 4, pp. 303–21.

Thurik, A. (2009). 'Entreprenomics: entrepreneurship, economic growth and policy'. In Z. J. Acs, D. B. Audretsch and R. Strom (eds), *Entrepreneurship, growth, and public policy*, Cambridge University Press, pp. 219–49.

Timmons J. A. (1997). *New venture creation: entrepreneurship in the 21st century.* McGraw Hill.

Resources

Shell LiveWIRE – www.shell-livewire.org
Team Insight – www.team-insight.co.uk
The Prince's Trust – www.princes-trust.org.uk

4 Creating Opportunities and Spotting Them

Creating and spotting opportunities is the cornerstone of success for young entrepreneurs. We have all met someone at a party who has boasted of an idea they are convinced will make them millions. Six months later they are saying the same thing. The gutsy few actually make it happen. Entrepreneurs have an idea, gather the necessary information, assess it and then go for it. Shane (2003) suggests that entrepreneurship occurs when a prepared individual meets a suitable opportunity. As I. M. Kirzner put it in 1973 (Deakins and Freel, 2009), entrepreneurship is the ability to perceive new opportunities. Young entrepreneurs should be alert to spotting opportunities. J. A. Schumpeter in 1934 (cited in Deakins and Freel, 2009) described the entrepreneur as a special person, an innovator who brings change through new technological processes or products. Drucker (1985) argues that entrepreneurs take advantage of opportunities for change and creation. Entrepreneurs are constantly searching for change and then responding to it, they exploit it as an opportunity.

They may see opportunities when others see chaos (for example, F. H. Knight, 1921, cited in Deakins and Freel, 2009). They may view the world in a different way to others but they are not usually reckless risk-takers. They are calculated risk-takers, as discussed in Chapter 3. They don't take unnecessary risks. They are also well networked and surround themselves with people who can do the day-to-day management of the business while they focus on their strengths. Shackle describes an entrepreneur as someone who gambles on his or her imagination (Deakins and Freel, 2012). Opportunity-centred entrepreneurship is an active learning process stimulated by curiosity, desire and the intention to find out something and achieve results (Rae, 2014). Solveiga Pakštaitė illustrates this beautifully.

Solveiga Pakštaitė – Design by Sol

Quirky, confident and intelligent Solveiga Pakštaitė, the 22-year-old founder of Design by Sol, is easily recognisable with her inimitable trademark glasses and bags of confidence. This, together with her intelligence and tenacity in finding solutions, won her the coveted James Dyson Award for her Bump Mark innovation while still an undergraduate, catapulting her to a new league. The young Lithuanian developed a cost-effective technology that reduces the alarming problem of food waste. Bump Mark tells you the exact condition of food inside the packaging simply by running your finger over the label. This reluctant entrepreneur has travelled far and wide with her innovation and went on to be a winner for Shell LiveWIRE Smarter Future programme for her Design by Sol Company.

Born in Norway to Lithuanian parents, Solveiga Pakštaitė grew up in England. Both her parents are academics so it was no surprise that Solveiga went on to study for a Bachelor of Arts in Industrial Design and Technology at the University of Brunel. This degree required all students to complete a final-year project. Solveiga excelled in hers with her Bump Mark technology and was soon on her road to entrepreneurship, albeit reluctantly.

So, how did Solveiga come up with the idea for the project in the first place? It came about in a typically entrepreneurial way – when she tried to solve a problem.

Bump Mark came about when Solveiga did a placement year between her second and final year. She was working for a design and ergonomics consultancy, and one of the projects she worked on was Guide Dogs for the Blind Association. She spent six months talking to blind people almost every day. The project was about access to public transport but she found herself fascinated by her subjects and pondered on other issues as she conducted her interviews and travel observations. Her curiosity got the better of her and she would ask them questions such as, 'how do you measure how much milk goes in your tea?' They had a gadget for that and Solveiga was impressed. She then asked, 'how do you match your clothes?' and 'they'd always have a cool answer', she recalls. One day she asked, 'how do you know when your food goes off?' There was no answer. They said, 'we don't!' Solveiga prompted them further: 'Oh come on you must have a cool gadget for that?', but they did not. Exasperated

Solveiga said, 'so you know how much milk to put in your tea but you don't know if that milk is off or not?' and the response was 'no!' Solveiga was horrified. She knew then that she would investigate this further when she returned for her final year at university. It was a problem that was so interesting she determined that this was going to be the topic for her final-year project.

'I had no idea how I was going to do it. Absolutely none', she confesses. Resolute, she started exploring lots of avenues. She was looking into whether the solution could be something via audio or touch. She soon became an expert on gadgets for the blind and her business brain was on alert. She was smart enough to realise that anything she could develop for this group would not be attractive for any potential commercial buyer as the production runs would be too small and thus not viable. Solveiga realised, 'because it's for a specific group of people, each unit costs a lot more to make up with the tooling costs and that actually prohibits the very people who you've designed it for'. It would be too expensive for them to buy given that only a third of blind people are in paid employment, and the other two-thirds, Solveiga explains, 'are actually living on the poverty mark so it's a big, vicious cycle'. There was no way to benefit from economies of scale. She had to change tactics and was determined to create a solution that would add value for the mass market.

Life gets better as you get older unless you're a banana

Solveiga ruthlessly went through the options: 'I threw out audio straight away because you need to use electronics and it was just going to be far too expensive. I kept thinking, "what else can I do?"' It was the humble banana that was to lead to a solution. 'One day I was looking at a banana that I'd forgotten about and it was starting to go brown and the skin was starting to go a bit manky and I thought, "why doesn't our plastic packaging do that and let us know when it's on its way out?"' The banana, Solveiga observed, 'starts to go a bit knobbly'. It was a eureka moment. She became obsessed with this bumpy package appearance. Immediately she marched off to the material science department and told them, 'I need a material that changes its texture in reaction to food inside'. She was met with derision. 'They said "Are you crazy? It doesn't exist, it's a nice idea but that's it".'

'I realized then that I was barking up the wrong tree', she admits. She then went, armed with her banana, to speak to some biologists, chemists and people who she claims understood food decay. She wanted to know what material she could use to mimic the banana. 'One of the scientists said, "why don't you use gelatin?" My initial thought was "what?"' However, they explained: 'Because gelatin is a protein it can really match different meats well and it changes, it's a thermo reversible gel, meaning that it goes back to a liquid when it completely expires.' They advised her to look into it.

Solveiga went back to her lab where she saw her class working on chairs and furniture and cool devices, 'while I was in my kitchen playing with gelatin', she recalls. Eventually she got a layered structure to work, she explains, 'so as the gel goes bad it turns into a liquid and it removes this barrier that then lets you touch a bumpy layer, so it changes from smooth to bumpy'. Jubilant, she recalls proudly: 'So, yeah, I got that to work.'

This was particularly important because, apart from her supervisor, everyone who she turned to for advice would 'give me a half hour lecture and waste my whole meeting slot telling me that if they were my supervisor they would never have let me do this project', she recalls frustrated.

They did not see her burning passion and her desire to solve the problem. They reminded her that she should focus on getting a first-class degree rather than actually do something interesting for her project. She was annoyed: 'The reaction was – just go get a first class degree and get out, you're a good student.' Solveiga knew she was a good student but she passionately believed in her product and found the learning process really interesting; she was determined to continue until she found a solution. They warned her she might fail unless she dropped this nonsense, but undeterred she continued. 'I got a first class degree by the way', she declares proudly. 'I did make it work, but yeah it was interesting how I was encouraged to take the easy route.' The danger today is that, due to financial and other pressures students face, most are strategic about the modules they choose and how they complete them, always aiming for a good grade rather than the experience of learning. Solveiga broke the mould.

In short, Solveiga's final-year project was based on a bio-reactive food expiry label, 'which basically means that it's a label that you can gear up to act in the exact same way that food does and it actually experiences decay and then knows when your food goes off', she explains.

About two months into her project the students had an industrial review evening, where designers and other professionals from industry look at the students' initial concepts and offer advice. 'It's super, super, helpful', she exclaims. 'One of the guys I spoke to was a packaging designer and as soon as I started telling him about my idea, he said, "you need to protect this".' Solveiga was surprised: 'It was strange to hear that as I hadn't even finished the project!'

It was about this time that Solveiga, together with some other good students on her course, won a £1,000 scholarship, which was intended to cover the development of their product and to build prototypes. The other winners were in a different position financially because they were making prototypes using metal, wood, electronics and these materials are quite expensive, whereas Solveiga was playing with plastic and gelatin and so by the end of the year she still had her £1,000. She decided to take heed of the professional advice she had been offered and file a patent. 'Even if nothing happens with it I'll know a bit more about intellectual property', she reasoned, viewing the process as a learning experience.

The next stage of the project was a graduate show where students had to display their work to experts from the industry. Here, Solveiga met Kristina Rayko, who develops technologies to commercialisation. Kristina was impressed with Solveiga's work and asked if she had protected her intellectual property. Eagerly, Solveiga said, 'Yes, I filed for a UK patent two weeks ago!' Kristina was impressed and straight away explained that she worked in intellectual property and commercialisation, and could find Solveiga some initial funding and introduce her to the right people. 'Let's make this thing happen!', Kristina said.

Solveiga found herself in a strong position. She had someone interested in her innovation who was an expert in commercialising high-tech products, but Solveiga was still unsure of her own business acumen, wanting instead to sell her idea and let someone else run the business. 'I'm not interested in running a company. I kept telling Kristina, I don't want to run a company.'

Reluctant entrepreneur

Solveiga had never intended to be an entrepreneur, expecting to follow the professional route. 'I didn't want to be an entrepreneur', she asserts, fearing she would lose her creative potential. 'It sounded like my idea of hell because I didn't understand it.' What Solveiga had not appreciated was that by owning her own company she did not have to stop being the creative person who does the design work: 'I thought you would be bogged down with numbers and things like that.' What she had not realised is that she could appoint someone else to be the CEO and take care of the business side.

But even when Solveiga made that realisation, 'I still didn't want to start my own company,' she claims, fearing the idea. Yet fate can play a lot of tricks, and sometimes an opportunity taken can change your life. She had been working on her final-year project at university and was now 'sick of it'. She had put in too many hours and just wanted to finish her degree. However, all her colleagues were entering their projects for the James Dyson Awards, an international design award inspiring the next generation of design engineers. Solveiga rationalised, 'it's free to enter, it only takes ten minutes to write up an application so I did it'. She then forgot all about it and started her first graduate job: 'I was just going to do the normal thing, follow a career path.'

A landmark event was to put a different spin on her life. 'I ended up winning the UK James Dyson Award!' she exclaims. The press went crazy. Solveiga became a minor celebrity and companies started approaching her, inviting her to meetings. 'It happened accidentally; it wasn't a choice I made.' She did, however, have to decide whether to pursue these opportunities or not: 'I thought it would be idiotic not to, so, yes!'

Solveiga received £2,000 from the James Dyson Award. More importantly she received a tremendous amount of media attention: 'I was working as an intern and I was sneaking off to meetings with Coca-Cola executives in my lunch break. It was ridiculous!' she recalls. By the end of the year, her internship company were keen to extend her contract but by then Solveiga was ready to take a leap of faith and concentrate on her business. 'I'm going to see where this goes and that was terrifying', she recalls.

Solveiga formed a company, Design by Sol, and appointed Kristina Rayko as the CEO. Solveiga appreciates what Kristina has brought to the company with her strategic consultancy background and strength in writing grant applications: 'She's very, very smart. A good person to have on board and we still work together today.' They are developing new products as well as Bump Mark.

So, albeit with trepidation, Solveiga resolved to take the plunge. What made her change her mind was the enormous experience she was gaining from the attention surrounding her Bump Mark innovation. She was being thrown into meetings with these huge companies, having to present her idea as a venture and realised: 'I'm probably going to learn way more than any of my friends sitting in their junior design positions.' She was not afraid of failure. 'Even if this whole thing falls flat on its face at least I would have learnt so much.' Once she resolved to commit to the business she gave it her full attention. Solveiga advises that you have to go into business with total commitment: 'There's no point doing it half heartedly, nothing's going to happen.'

The company is still developing the technology and has financed itself through grants. Solveiga is confident about the future, as there are several companies lined up who are interested in the product.

Attracting money

Solveiga, with the benefit of Kristina's expertise, has concentrated on awards and grants, and the novelty and usefulness of her technology have meant that she has had great success in getting funding. In terms of finance, her biggest grants have been from the government: 'Innovate UK are definitely the ministry for giving technology companies money; it's fantastic!' she claims. Initially, she received an Innovation Voucher, which she explains, 'pays for someone else to help you start off, which was basically Kristina's salary for six months, so that was around £5,000'. She continues: 'And then there were awards that we entered, so I won the Mayor of London's Low Carbon Entrepreneur prize. It was supposed to be £20,000 but they picked a runner-up so I only got £15,000.'

Solveiga also receives funding through her involvement with an incubator at Imperial College: 'It's called Climate-KIC and it's funded by 250 institutions and companies throughout Europe.' They give money to help sustainable, carbon-reducing companies and it is a three-stage process, so she received 20,000 euros for Stage 1 and is now ready for her Stage 2 funding. More importantly: 'They do this fantastic thing where they send you to different master classes. You get Harvard business school people teaching you how to run a marketing campaign and that kind of thing. So the education value is huge from that as well.' All in all, Solveiga explains proudly, 'to date we've raised over £80,000 from different grants and competitions and that kind of thing'. The product is poised to hit the market with a bang!

What social life?

The business has an enormous impact on Solveiga's work-life balance. The business cuts into her social life and remains her first priority: 'I put in about 12 hours a day.' It is a hectic schedule, with some weeks more frantic than others. 'I love the flexibility of it', she admits. 'If there's something going on in the middle of the day I can just go to it and then make up the time in the evening.' Responding quickly and being flexible is something that she has learnt to master: 'I was invited to speak at a conference in Hong Kong and because I didn't have a nine to five to go back to I stayed on for an extra four days to see the sights.' That freedom makes up for the long hours in the business.

She likes the variety too: 'I think when you're having a very important and productive meeting, but it's in a pub on the Thames, you're thinking, "this is great" … it doesn't feel like work because it's so exciting and exhilarating. The more you do the more you learn.'

Her family are proud of her achievements and were really excited about her winning the James Dyson Award; however, when she broke the news to them that she wasn't going back to work after her internship, 'they were terrified!' she recalls. 'They're both university teachers so it's a completely different world.' They had the usual concerns of, 'who's going to pay your salary?' I said, 'well, technically me but I'm not going to pay myself yet, 'which did nothing to dampen their concerns!' she proclaims ruefully.

Luckily for Solveiga she has found her mentor in Kristina as she concedes: 'I think my parents felt bad that they can't give me any advice because they have literally no clue and there's no one in my family that I can turn to for free advice really.' They have adjusted to her new career status now. 'They see it as less of a big deal because they just see it as my job and luckily I'm setting up my first ever payroll, so good things are happening.'

Not one to just tick boxes, Solveiga thinks outside the box and is confident and resolute enough to carry on until she succeeds. Less confident students would have given up and taken the easy route, but she persevered and believed in her own convictions: 'Even through school, whenever we got a project I'd always try to think of an interesting way of doing it and I sometimes didn't even get good grades because I didn't tick the boxes, but I've always hated doing that. So I guess in a way, being an entrepreneur has always suited me, I just didn't realize it!'

Solveiga's advice for wannabees is: 'If it's a product, then my top advice is enter into some competitions, because you'd get the best feedback ever.' She continues: 'If you win, you know it's a good idea and it takes a lot of the risk out and you're already going in saying I've won this award.' It is the best way of getting honest feedback and it's a good testing ground. She also advises that you should try to go to events within that area: 'So if you've designed something like a bone conducting headphone or something like that, then go to some audio conventions and then just say, "Hey so I've been doing some research into bone conduction for music, what do you think?"' Just getting a conversation started with other professionals is important. Finally: 'Don't just blindly go and start a company. You really need to see if there's some interest there first. So I think the easiest way in terms of products is entering competitions and just chatting to people within that field and if you get good responses from that, absolutely go for it, you will learn so much.'

Summary

Solveiga is an intelligent woman who enjoys the thrill of learning new things as she relentlessly looks for ways forward. She is determined and headstrong, gnawing away at a problem until she finds a solution, and often looking outside the box. Unabashed, she put herself forward for competitions and set herself up for success. She created her own opportunities, and meetings with professionals were not wasted when they came to view her products. She took heed of their advice, applying for a patent to protect her product, which is a must according to Southon and West (2002). She attracted the interest of her now-CEO who has proved a successful mentor to work with. Solveiga is no shrinking violet; she has taken control of her destiny, growing and learning along the way. Opportunities don't just come to you – you need to give them a nudge sometimes.

For more information and to watch an interview with Solveiga Pakštaitė, please visit our companion website at www.he.palgrave.com/dhaliwal-millionaire.

Key learnings

- Stay alert to opportunities
- Think creatively
- Win awards
- Have a scalable business
- Protect your idea
- Commit to your business wholeheartedly.

References

Deakins, D. and M. Freel (2012). *Entrepreneurship and small firms*. McGraw Hill, pp. 4–6.

Drucker, P. F. (1985). 'Entrepreneurial strategies', *California Management Review*, vol. 27, no. 2, pp. 9–25.

Rae, D. (2014). *Opportunity-centred entrepreneurship*. Palgrave Macmillan.

Shane, S, (2003). *A general theory of entrepreneurship*. Edward Elgar.

Southon, M. and C. West (2002). *The beermat entrepreneur*. Pearson. Prentice Hall.

Resources

Climate-KIC – www.climate-KIC.org

Design by Sol – www.designbysol.co.uk

James Dyson Award – www.jamesdysonaward.org

Innovate UK – www.gov.uk/government/organisations/innovate-uk

Mayor of London's Low Carbon Entrepreneur prize – www.london.gov.uk/what-we-do/environment/green-economy/mayor-londons-low-carbon-entrepreneur-2016

5 Universities – What Works Best?

Universities are the perfect breeding ground for young entrepreneurs. They offer a safe environment to experiment with ideas and to seek help and direction. When students are paying over £9,000 plus per year for their degree, they need something to believe in and aspire to other than the burden of debt on completion. Enterprise offers this hope.

Entrepreneurship is present in the curriculum in almost all universities in the UK, according to a study by Tosey *et al.* (2011). Student-run businesses are actively encouraged, and are provided with support through a wide variety of programmes, competitions and grants aimed at fostering enterprise and entrepreneurship among students. In many universities, centres of enterprise and entrepreneurship or special interest groups have been established to encourage students, faculty members and members of the local community to create new enterprises and to develop existing enterprises. Programmes related to these initiatives include coaching for would-be entrepreneurs, seed funding grants, competitions, enterprise summer schools and more.

There are some great examples of innovative practices (Tosey *et al.*, 2011). The University of Buckingham's two-year BSc in Business Enterprise offers an undergraduate programme in which it is possible for participants to start and run their own business and has attracted some great international students.

A novel approach is offered by the Finnish Team Academy founded in Jyvaskala, Finland, which promotes a really different form of business degree. Its students are called 'team entrepreneurs'. There are no classrooms but open-plan offices, no teachers but coaches, and no simulations but learning through creating and running real businesses (Tosey, Dhaliwal and Hassinen, 2015).

The Team Academy model involves undergraduates in a full-time, three-and-a-half-year degree programme. The student teams are coached and mentored by faculty members and the emphasis is on experiential learning, reflection and peer and self-assessment. The Universities of the West of England, Falmouth and Northumbria have adopted this approach and the University of Westminster will launch this too in September 2016.

Universities need to create environments for students to have these experiences and learn from them. Facing a job interview or pitching a business idea once you have experienced risk and failure many times over is much easier. Failure can be a good thing; it pushes you forward. In many countries, failure is simply not part of the culture, and this is even more so in academia where league tables often set the agenda. In the US, failure of enterprise is accepted. The expectation is that you will probably have failed at least three times before you have a successful venture. In the UK, if you fail you are deemed a failure.

Employability and enterprise go hand in hand. Students need to be aware of the world of work and ensure that they develop skills while studying. Professor Heather McLaughlin from Canterbury Christchurch University says: 'We have employability tutors instead of personal tutors, where students are guided on writing CVs (*Curricula Vitae*) and other useful skills.' This equips them far better for employment and self-employment prospects.

For enterprise to be part of university culture, it needs many stakeholders; alumni can play a big role and so can enterprise societies. The National Association of College and University Entrepreneurs (NACUE) aims to make the next generation more entrepreneurial than ever before through their network of over 32,000 students in 260 colleges and universities across the UK. 'NACUE gives college and university students the opportunity to boost their skills, confidence and aspirations through student-led enterprise societies, practical programmes and inspiring events. We are powering the enterprising generation, encouraging them to put their ideas into action to gain the capability they'll need to thrive in an ever changing future economy', says Johnny Luk, NACUE Chief Executive.

So what makes a good student society?

University entrepreneurship societies are gaining a lot of momentum and are responsible for sowing the seeds of enterprise in young people. Entrepreneurial societies are vital in terms of creating new entrepreneurs and instilling life skills. Students may just want to use that space to build skills such as teamwork, communication, leadership and building confidence. A good society needs to be free from excessive student politics; it should be accessible to all and cross-faculty, have a good relationship with academic staff and have the support of the university to enable things to happen. Societies need not be expensive to run; you just need access to a room, as most speakers will attend for free to inspire students. Societies must add value to the student experience and also enhance the reputation of the institution.

It's a great opportunity to experiment. If universities are safe places to fail, then this is a chance to be a risk-taker and learn from the experience. It should include a wide range of subjects, so think outside the box and put economists together with biologists, engineers and dance and drama students to create an innovative mix. Students need to generate, evaluate and execute ideas.

Universities can work alongside other organisations such as the charity Young Enterprise who have a Start Up programme for university students designed to couple academic rigour with practical applications culminating in a European Final competition. This empowers students to 'unleash creativity, and embeds the skills, attitudes and behaviours needed by industry today' (www.young-enterprise.org.uk).

The National Union of Students (NUS) is looking at how to move away from being run like an amateur charity and become more like a professional social enterprise. This would mean changes to the way clubs and societies are run at universities. Do you ask for a grant each year or do you present a business case?

Perhaps enterprise education should be all-inclusive. Students must behave in entrepreneurial ways. They need to be agile and quick to respond to change. An employable graduate may not be enterprising but an enterprising graduate will be employable. Entrepreneurship is an ability to navigate complex situations, to spot opportunities and to take opportunities. Here's one young entrepreneur who went to university with a purpose.

Sarah Watkinson-Yull – Yull Shoes

One example of an entrepreneur who used opportunities for entrepreneurship at university is Sarah Watkinson-Yull, the founder of Yull Shoes. Sarah has turned traditional education on its head. Most graduates start studying and then decide what career they want to pursue in their final year. Sarah flipped the system by starting her business at the age of 18 and then doing a degree to see how it would help her business. Because of this she was learning with a purpose, based on her business needs, for profit. She was a committed and motivated student who has set the trend for the way ahead for many of today's students. Below we see how Sarah took charge of her life.

A lover of fashion, Sarah completed a foundation course in fashion at the London College of Fashion before going to the University of Westminster where she studied as an undergraduate in Business Management, majoring in Entrepreneurship.

Sarah had nine shoe designs under her belt when she embarked on her undergraduate degree: 'I wanted to set up my own website whilst I was at university.' For Sarah, her business and education journey went hand in hand as she started getting her shoes manufactured in China just as her degree began. Although Sarah's real desire was to own a British company, she used Chinese manufacturers initially to keep her costs down. She had looked for suppliers and manufacturers in the UK but none were available to her. The response to her from the British Footwear Association was, 'you'll never find anyone making high heeled shoes for ladies'. Sarah explains: 'We have a big industry in the UK for men's shoes but for high heels everyone goes to Italy, Spain or Portugal.' Finally, in her second year at university, after six months of trying to find a manufacturer, a jubilant Sarah announced: 'I found someone who was happy to split the costs!' She was delighted. This meant, however, that she needed money to start the venture and for this she approached The Prince's Trust and received a loan to start manufacturing her design of shoes in England.

Sarah feels she was destined to be an entrepreneur. 'Both my parents are entrepreneurs, so that was a great help', she recalls. 'I sort of grew up in an entrepreneurial household; it was always what I wanted to do.' She had a clarity of purpose; Sarah wanted to be her own boss: 'I like the freedom of the lifestyle that you can get from it. I'm very bossy and I hate being told what to do, so I wouldn't be the best employee.'

At university Sarah was focused: 'I worked jolly hard, I didn't have much time to do anything else.' Unlike many of her peers who had left home for the first time and were enjoying their social life, Sarah had a maturity beyond her years. She had gone to university to learn how to progress her business, 'I was very fortunate at the university, loads of my modules were all based around the business so I was able to combine study with business and they really complemented each other.'

So how did she get into shoes?

'From the age of 16, before I did my foundation course, I really knew I wanted to go into fashion', Sarah explains. She worked for a big footwear company in north London and then worked for Topshop in their shoe department and she knew she wanted to study fashion and take it seriously. Her focus on shoes was clear from the start and her business idea got an early boost: 'When I was studying fashion I won a competition for Doc Martens and that was all about shoes and I was working at Harrods and it was with shoes and I did all my fashion projects on shoes.' She was becoming an expert on the subject. Sarah knew her market and was abreast of the latest developments. In short, she knew all about shoes.

Having built up all this knowledge: 'I was like, oh well, I'm going to have go into shoes because I don't know about anything else now.' The die was cast. Sarah had always been resolute about working for herself: 'I knew I wanted to start my own shoe company and then I went and worked for a year to save up money and that's when I went to university and started the business.'

Shoestring budget

In the early stages Sarah used the money she had saved up from working and that paid for her initial stock and the website. However, after that, she recalls: 'I was a bit screwed because I'd spent all the money and you always need more money when you're starting a business.' Her next step was to take a loan from The Prince's Trust and that went towards the manufacturing costs in the UK. Always on the lookout for opportunities and convinced of the quality of her product Sarah then won a grant from the European Development Fund. 'It was only £500 but that helped tremendously in the early days', she explains. Since then she has been awarded another grant from the Manufacturing

Advisory Services to the tune of £560. Sarah continues: 'And then I've had other grants from the UKTI [UK Trade and Industry] when I go and do trade shows overseas. So, in total, I think funding I've had is probably about £8,000 or £9,000.' Sarah did her homework and found out the best fit with organisations that could help her business financially.

Most students go to university, they study and then they decide what they're going to do. Sarah started her business and used her degree to build up her business. This not only helped with her creativity and future career path but also made her a better student; she wanted more from the modules she studied. It was important, not just for her grades, but for her learning and potential to make profits. She was a student with a purpose: 'I felt I was a better student because I was really engaged and I really needed help.' Sarah continues: 'I knew I didn't really know much, so I was really asking tutors, what about this? what about that? how do I do that?' More importantly, she could apply all that she learnt: 'I felt like it really helped because I had a foundation to base all the ideas you were learning at university.'

Sarah's practical work experience also was a big plus: 'Having worked for a year I think that also really helped because it's all well and good learning the theory but I think that you can't really learn something until you've really been able to apply it.' The result is: 'I learnt so much more at university because I was able to apply it all and I learnt by working rather than, oh this is the theory and then you forget it and then you're in a workplace and then you suddenly go, oh my God what was it that tutor was talking about, and you go back to your notes and you go, oh yes, I can see how that would be applied, but I think I really was able to learn it because I was applying it all the time.'

Despite been so focused and resourceful, she faced many challenges as all new businesses do. 'I was starting a brand, being completely unknown, quite a few people probably thinking you're a bit mental, but then that's most entrepreneurs.' Carving a name for herself was a major hurdle, and she was uncertain as to what to do. 'I just jumped at every opportunity, went and did everything, so I think sort of not knowing the correct way to do things is quite a big challenge.' Her youth was an initial hindrance. 'Being quite young is a challenge because people don't trust the business if it's just you as an individual, a 21-year-old, they're not exactly going to buy from you. It's quite difficult.' She had to overcome these hurdles and had to get people to trust and buy from her. Her advice is: 'Just to do your best and work really hard.'

Sarah is trying to build up her customer base but is wary of costs. 'I'm doing it as cheaply as possible.' She has a company that works on PR for her. 'I do a lot on social media.' Her business cannot afford any paid advertising but she explains: 'Trade shows are great. Getting agents as well is a good way to be able to build on that.'

Her shoes are unique, colourful, playful and stylish. 'I have a pair called the Chelsea Flower Shoe ... it's got some flowers at the back and is handmade in London.' It's an internationally sourced product. The leather is from England but the components are from Spain. 'I tried to get them made in England but the ones that are made in England were just not up to standard so I got all the components from Spain', Sarah explains.

Sarah designs the shoes, outsources the different materials and then manufactures in the UK. She keeps a careful watch at every stage: 'They're all made in the factory here in London so I'm there constantly overseeing it all, telling them what to do, driving them crazy.' They are then sold on her website and to small independent shops 'at the moment we've got stockists in Taiwan, Australia, America, right the way across Europe, Austria, Belgium, France, Germany, Italy and the UK', she explains. The business has done well. 'We're making a profit. But obviously we want to put as much money back into the business as possible to help it grow in these early days.'

The business is time-consuming, and unlike many of her peers who left university with a degree and are now enjoying their 20-something life-style, Sarah confesses the business takes up 'lots and lots of time'. She is constantly working hard but confesses she loves it and does not envy her peers for their chosen route: 'Well, I think that in about five years' time they'll all be saying that they want to start their own business, they hate having to work for somebody and, yeah, they'll probably be like, I wish I did it when I was young.' She admits she could never work for anyone else. 'It's the last thing I want to do. That's what drives me to be an entrepreneur, thinking how bad it would be having to go and work for someone and to abide by their rules.'

Sarah's best quality as an entrepreneur is efficiency, she explains: 'I do everything on time. I have good time management skills. I'm always striving for more. I think that's very important. I never settle, I'm always thinking about the next thing and everyone says, "oh you've done so well so far", and I'm like no, no, no, it's the next step now, I always want to keep pushing and pushing.'

Confident, mature, hard-working and efficient as Sarah is, who does she turn to for advice? 'I had a mentor through The Prince's Trust and that was for three years; I had a meeting with her once a month and she was constantly with me.' Sarah recalls: 'It helped so much in the early days, the first three years.' She is still in touch with her mentor now. 'I still get help from her from time to time. I think only about two weeks ago I was on the phone to her saying I don't know what to do about this, can you help me?' Sarah elaborates: 'That is the hardest thing; it's about not knowing.' It is tough having to make decisions. Sarah recalls: 'At university there was one module we did called Making Management Decisions and I always think that was such a good module because that is what business is all about; it's always about making decisions; you don't have all the knowledge but you have to make the decision to the best of your knowledge.' Her family are extremely important for advice too. 'My parents have been there and done that and got the T-shirt.'

Sarah is an active networker. 'I think going to trade shows is good because obviously I know lots of people in the industry all in the same boat.' She continues: 'There's a trade show called Best of Britannia so everyone gets stuff made in the UK, so that's quite a good network.' Sarah is becoming known in her market. 'The shoe industry in the UK is very small and it is pretty friendly so everyone tends to know each other.'

What is Sarah's advice to young people who are thinking of starting a business? 'I think be in it for the long run. Don't go into business because you want to make lots of money. If you want to make lots of money go and work in the City. I think if you're really passionate about what you do and you have the drive behind it that you enjoy it then I think you should do it.'

Sarah has made a name for herself as a fledgling shoe designer with her own range of shoes and is waving the flag for the UK. 'I'm hoping to go into other things; we've started making a few clutch bags to complement the shoes, made in England. I've got a perfume designed in Paris already so we're hoping to launch that soon as well and small accessories as well.' There is no stopping this dynamo; Sarah wants her shoes stocked in shops across the globe.

Summary

Sarah had the energy and drive for her business and her education to go hand in hand, thus raising her standards in both areas. She is passionate about her business and about flying the flag for Britain. Her hands-on approach and her care and attention at every step of the business process have held her in good stead and she is gaining a reputation in the fashion world. Sarah was smart enough to see which organisations could offer her help and grants, and this was essential for the business in the early days.

Universities are good breeding grounds for entrepreneurship. You can have some time at university to go and play, make mistakes and reflect on the skills you're developing. Sarah started her university education with her business. The modules she studied were put into practice and she grew by asking challenging questions of her tutors so she could push forward with her business.

For more information and to watch an interview with Sarah Watkinson-Yull, please visit our companion website at www.he.palgrave.com/dhaliwal-millionaire.

Key learnings

- Have passion and be in it for the long run
- Know your product and market and oversee production
- Develop your networks
- Go to trade shows
- Learn from mentors, academics and peers and use your university education to enhance your business
- Grow from your mistakes.

References

Robinson, G., N. Biggs, S. Dhaliwal, R. Happonen and P. Tosey (2011). *An exploration of the use of student-run, real businesses in the South East region, the UK and internationally for all or part of the award of a university degree.* Project Report: The Higher Education Entrepreneurship Group (HEEG), http://westminsterresearch.wmin. ac.uk/12630/, date accessed 1 July 2015.

Tosey, P., S. Dhaliwal and J. Hassinen (2015). 'The Finnish Team Academy model: implications for management education', *Management Learning*, vol. 46, no. 2, pp. 175–94.

Resources

European Development Fund – www.ec.europa.eu

Manufacturing Advisory Services – www.mas.businessgrowthservice.greatbusiness.gov.uk

National Association of College and University Entrepreneurs – www.nacue.com

National Union of Students (NUS) – www.nus.org.uk

The Prince's Trust – www.princes-trust.org.uk

UK Trade and Industry (UKTI) – www.gov.uk/government/organisations/uk-trade-investment

Young Enterprise – www.young-enterprise.org.uk

Yull – www.yull.co.uk

6 Graduate Businesses – Some Great Ideas

More and more graduates are considering starting a business than ever before. According to the Higher Education Statistics Agency some 52,000 undergraduates in the UK have set up a company within six months of leaving university, and these businesses range from marketing to information technology and fashion design.

It would seem that graduates today want their independence. A recent survey conducted by Enterprise Nation with Direct Line Insurance revealed that 15 per cent of undergraduates plan to set up their own firm on graduation. Students are turning their backs on corporate life and the main reason is they want to be their own boss. They also believe they can make more money on their own. They are worried about available job opportunities and concerned about low pay, job security and zero-hour contracts. These are a reality for today's graduates who are paying at least £9,000 a year tuition fees for three years in England and Wales, and many leave with well over £30,000 debt. They do not want to take up low-skilled jobs after all that.

So what sort of businesses are they starting and how do they come up with their ideas? In this chapter we look at two entrepreneurs who started businesses towards the end of their undergraduate degrees. The two entrepreneurs are very different in terms of their journey and the type of businesses they have started, but they both benefited from university life. Many good ideas come from the problems students have faced themselves. Frustration can get the imagination working and create solutions for the worst of problems. Take a look at Kristian Else.

Kristian Else – Hallbookers.co.uk

Australian Kristian Else, at the tender age of 21, founded hallbookers. co.uk, a student accommodation review website. Melbourne-born Kristian, like thousands of overseas students who come to study in the UK every year, was horrified with his accommodation. Living in substandard halls was a nightmare, but he had a university to settle into, assignments to complete and money to worry about, as well as three years of undergraduate life to get through. Frustrated, but not one to suffer in silence, he turned his problem into a business opportunity, giving a voice to students so they can warn others of the reality of their private accommodation. His focus is on providing a service and giving a voice to those that are vulnerable when they arrive. Kristian has challenged the status quo and turned his problem into an attractive business proposition, which has attracted both media attention and financiers to back him.

Kristian had hankered after being an entrepreneur for a long time. 'I've always had in the back of my mind that I wanted to start my own business.' He came to the UK to study Business Management at the University of Westminster and enjoyed his degree. 'It really gave an introduction into entrepreneurship and an introduction into business in general', he affirms. 'The main thing I took away from it was learning the terminology of business, being able to speak the business language and communicate with people that way.'

However, it was when he came to London and started working at a shop in King's Cross station that his desire for freedom became a priority. 'I had a really horrible boss', he states. He was working in a chocolate shop and his boss did not respect any of his initiatives. Annoyed, Kristian reflected on the situation: 'I didn't like her at all, and I realised that I was working for this company that were making huge profits and I was getting paid about £6.50 per hour.' This was particularly difficult in Central London where the cost of living is so high.

This was the turning point, but worse was yet to come: 'I got robbed overseas and I lost a whole ton of my stuff and I realised that at £6.50 an hour it's going to take me years to buy back all my stuff.' He knew then that he did not want to be working in low-paid jobs to get by: 'so that's when it really started to kick in that I wanted to become an entrepreneur', and, he continues, 'I started to pursue it in my own way'. He began by reading books, exploring ideas, 'basic stuff like Richard Branson's books, and then I started to develop ideas about businesses'. The more he read and thought about it, the more and more motivated he got to start his own business. It got his brain cells turning: 'I'd started to switch my brain on to start coming up with business ideas, and it got to the point where I would have a booklet of ideas that I'd write on every day and pretty much come up with two or three ideas every day.' He carried on building up this list: 'After about six months I had a list of a whole ton of ideas.' He was bursting to start a business, but which one?

His business was to come from his personal need. Like most overseas students he stayed in private student accommodation in his first year of university: 'I had a horrible experience', he recalls vividly, 'and just noticed that there was a huge issue with students getting ripped off by landlords'. His accommodation was substandard, he felt unsafe and the landlords took the rent but did not keep their side of the bargain in terms of standard and repairs. His accommodation was so different from the glossy brochures he had seen in Melbourne, and he really felt he had been cheated. This was at a time when he was settling into his new university and starting his degree. 'It was a traumatic year!' he recalls.

However, he was alert to opportunities: 'It was about a year later when I started brainstorming business ideas it really hit me that this was a huge opportunity. I could create a business out of that, and solve that problem. I could give students the power over their hall providers, over the landlords.' Kristian was excited; he was determined to turn a negative into a positive and to give students a voice: 'There was a great purpose behind it and it was a great business opportunity, as well.'

Financing the business

Kristian began his business with money from Start Up Loans UK, a government-backed scheme which provides advice, loans and mentoring to start-up businesses. 'They gave me about £9,000', he explains. It was just enough to build a proof of concept for the website (a proof of concept demonstrates the feasibility of a service). 'At the time I thought that £9,000 was more than enough to create a sustainable, long-term business, but I was quite naïve when I started it', he admits, confessing that he had trouble writing the business plan for this opportunity.

Kristian explains: 'Start Up Loans was quite interesting actually because it was a rare investment opportunity.' He continues: 'It was a great thing, because they don't judge you on what you've done in the past and they don't really judge you on what you are capable of at that time. I think they saw a bit of enthusiasm in me and they saw a business plan that was absolutely horribly written at the time, but they still gave me the opportunity to go ahead with it, just because, I guess, they saw it as an opportunity for me to use that money to grow and learn, and that's what I did.' Kristian was aware that he would have to pay the money back and so this added to his determination to succeed.

He worked hard but was overwhelmed with the task at hand and had underestimated it. He also had to work part-time to support himself during this period.

Kristian's business took a huge turn for the better when the London *Evening Standard* ran an article about him. This was the breakthrough Kristian needed. 'Some investor got in touch with me and said it's a great concept and that they wanted to get involved', he explains. He must have been convincing because they invested £75,000 and gave the business the impetus it needed. His financier was already in the student accommodation industry, so he knew the market. 'They could see that it was a great opportunity and it was something that was really needed', Kristian explains proudly.

His financier was experienced in real estate and together with Kristian they built up the business plan. 'He gave me a lot of guidance on which way to take it. At the time I was quite lost', Kristian confesses. 'Well, it was coming to a stage where I didn't really know what the next stage was after that. I definitely wasn't making the most of the potential of the idea. I should have been trying to get investments, really push things forward before another competitor came in.' Kristian was lucky that he met his financier and mentor when he did. 'He came in at a very good time, gave me the guidance to push things forward, and I think from there we really established ourselves as the UK student accommodation review website, and any competitors were behind us at that stage. They couldn't keep up!'

The business is built on the premise of creating value for students, and like a lot of tech start-ups, they don't really make a lot of money. Kristian's business is based on creating value first and profit later down the line. Kristian is employed by the company. 'I've got a standard wage, and my main intention is to hopefully grow the business, and that's the way I want to live.'

Challenges with the business

When asked about the challenges of the business, Kristian replies: 'I was really young, I had to learn a lot of things from scratch.' He had to develop a strategy for the business as well as consider the operation. 'There was digital marketing, there was a lot of reading, a lot of things along those lines.' The leap from student to entrepreneur was a huge one, and one that carries a lot of responsibility, particularly if you have borrowed money and have investors who expect you to deliver.

Kristian also confesses: 'I did not know what to do when I was initially approached by the investor, I had absolutely no idea, I've never had a business meeting with anyone in my life so it was quite a big step going into that.' He has gained experienced. 'Now I'm having business meetings with some of the operations directors of these huge companies, and it's a huge learning curve, I think that the hardest thing is how to communicate with people in a business meeting, how to really get things moving and build action points, these kind of things.'

Kristian says, 'the business has made a huge impact on my life, on my personal life'. This leaves him little room for any social life. 'It's standard that you work 70 hours a week, sometimes more, 80 hours a week. It's a part of your life.' This means there are things he must sacrifice. 'So, yeah, there's a lot you have to let go of, and you have to do that, but I've tried to position myself around people that are willing to work that hard in life so they understand that you can't always go out, you can't do these things, so it works out OK.'

His work ethic has changed. 'I used to be a very lazy student', he confesses. His original routine did not set him up for entrepreneurial success. 'When I first started the business I would wake up at about 2 o'clock in the afternoon, do about four hours of work.' This has had to change. It is a shock change from the student lifestyle. 'One of the hardest things I've had to develop is the ability to just have more energy and to go from doing about a 15-hour week to about a 70-hour, 80-hour week, so that's been a huge transition.'

His parents are very proud of him and supportive, although they are in Australia. They are entrepreneurs themselves but Kristian does not credit them as his only influence. 'I just always think of that boss that was horrible and that was pretty much it.'

So what advice would Kristian give to a current student or recent graduate who is thinking about launching a new business? 'The most important advice I could give is to really put a lot of effort into the brainstorming of creating a business. I think it's one of the most overlooked things.' People say they want to start a business, 'but there's very few places in the world where you can actually learn how to brainstorm effectively' and, he continues: 'I'm sure that some people create about four or five business ideas and start their business based on those ideas, which is far too small. You need to create at least 60, 70 business ideas before you get started.' Warming to his theme he goes on to explain: 'They call it the engine of your brain, the ideas engine in your brain, and you can switch it on and after a while of trying to brainstorm it becomes natural and it also becomes quite too much at some point because you're just constantly coming up with ideas, but it's definitely something you need to do if you're going to be an entrepreneur.'

But how do you know which idea to take forward? 'Well, I think for a young person or a student they should really put a lot of effort into it until they have a sort of eureka moment and they really know that it's going to work. There shouldn't be any doubt for a young person starting in business because they're already at a disadvantage because they've got no experience already, so if they haven't really come up with that eureka idea they need to just keep going, and they haven't done the brainstorming properly.'

Kristian picked something that was a problem for him. He had faced a difficulty with accommodation, saw an opportunity and wanted to give a voice to people who didn't really have a voice. Many international students come to London and find it is very expensive and this is compounded if they have poor accommodation at high prices. Kristian is passionate about helping them. 'You've got these landlords that are making a huge profit out of students that don't have a lot of money, and some of these companies are international corporations. And so it's always a great thing to start disrupting the market.' He wants students to feel safe and comfortable in accommodation that they are paying huge amounts for.

Perversely, his greatest strength as an entrepreneur is his myopia. 'I don't have a lot of foresight, which I think's been quite an advantage because if I did think things through too much I wouldn't have started the business because I definitely wasn't qualified to do it. It's one of those things, you just have to do it and see where it takes you. So, not over thinking things is always an advantage.' Kristian has certainly made a difference and many potential students can now rest assured that the reviews they read on his website provide real information from the experiences of other students. This has had an impact on the industry and landlords have had to raise their game.

For more information and to watch an interview with Kristian Else, please visit our companion website at www.he.palgrave.com/dhaliwal-millionaire.

Key learnings

- Turn your problems into business opportunities
- Look for creative solutions to problems and help others
- Get publicity
- Write a strong business plan
- Learn from experts
- Don't think too much – take action!
- Be prepared to devote all your time to the business
- Be professional – raise your game!

Another benefit of starting a business while, or just after, graduating is that you have a vast network of people to work with at university. Many academic assessments are now based on group work and so you can really tell who you get on with and who you can bounce ideas off. Nigel, our second entrepreneur in this chapter, met his business partner at university and went on to start up a creative business.

Nigel Westwood – Avelere

Universities are great places for study, but they're also great for finding future business partners. Nigel Westwood, the 22-year-old co-founder of Avelere, studied with Norwegian Guno Stuan before forming a business together straight after university. The Scandinavian influence plays a huge role in the style of Avelere, where they design and manufacture furniture and homewares. They put an interesting twist on furniture products and Nigel deals with outsourcing their manufacturing. They tried a few other businesses before Avelere, including handbag inserts which Nigel made himself and which helped finance Avelere. The hands-on entrepreneur recalls his journey to date.

No stranger to entrepreneurship, Nigel explains: 'My mum actually started a business when I was 10 and by 16, in my final year of school, I started working with her part-time.' By the time he finished school he took a year off and worked full-time with her. His mother ran a computer training business, 'so we'd basically go into larger companies and train them on Microsoft Office and that kind of thing', he recalls. This early influence planted the seed of entrepreneurship in his mind. 'I guess that kind of got me into the mindset that I could actually start my own business and run things when I went off to university.' In his final year at university he recalls: 'I was a bit short of money and I was doing a Business degree, so I was like, right I've got to start a business.' He explains: 'So I set up a website and just bought some stock, health supplement stuff, protein shakes and vitamins and things, and just started selling through this website.' This was an early taster of what was to come.

Nigel studied Business Administration at the University of Bath and originally was set to go into investment banking. He feels his degree did influence and motivate him to become an entrepreneur. 'I kind of focused mostly on finance and I did a couple of internships whilst I was at Bath working for different investment banks in London.' His entrepreneurship education was enriched when, in his final year, he went on an exchange to Simon Fraser University in Vancouver, Canada. Whilst he was there he focused exclusively on the entrepreneurship modules. This was a turning point for him. 'By that point I realised I don't really want to go into banking, I want to be starting my own business.'

He found the Canadian model of study more hands-on compared to the theoretical approach he had been used to in the UK. He enjoyed the Canadian approach: 'It was a lot more practical, they push you to come up with your own theories and draw on what other people have done but then try and take it somewhere else.'

Nigel met his business partner, Guro, at the University of Bath where they were studying together. They originally started another business. 'Guro is into fashion and she likes to buy designer handbags and those kind of things', Nigel explains, 'and she was going to buy this thing to go in the bottom of one of her handbags, they call it a base shaper. It's basically just a piece of acrylic plastic that's cut to the size of the bag to protect these £1,000 or so handbags … and she was going to buy one of these and it was £30 or something and I said I could make it for £5.' Nigel went and did just this. 'We started up this business together selling these base shapers online and then from there we've just carried on.'

He financed the base shapers business very cheaply. 'The money for that business was the last £100 of my student overdraft', Nigel recalls ruefully. Nigel knew basically what the product was and that it was quite easy to make, so telephoned several different plastics manufacturers until he found someone who was willing to send him one for free. This enabled him to check out the product, test it a bit and he effectively used his final £100 to get a small batch manufactured and delivered to his house. 'I think it was like ten of them and from there I agreed with the supplier that they'd supply us one by one as the orders came and send them direct out to our customers.' This was an excellent arrangement for the fledgling business and mitigated a lot of the risk. Nigel excelled at his organisation and negotiation skills, which would hold him in good stead for the challenges to come. He also understood the technical side of the product and thus could liaise with the manufacturers.

Explaining the product Nigel says, 'it's literally a sheet of acrylic plastic about 3mm thick cut to a very specific size to fit into the base of a handbag'. He continues: 'So that's how that started and from there we took some money from the base shapers business as it grew and put it into starting Avelere, which is our current company.'

At Avelere they make furniture and homeware goods. 'We make tables, chairs, little stools and so on, mostly out of wood at the moment, and also homeware products, such as scented candles, tea towels and so on.' They try and put a unique spin on everything they sell, 'so for example our furniture range is effectively like flat-pack, kind of Ikea-style, except everything goes together without screws, it just clips together. You can put it together with your hands, the idea is that it's very simple for people to do.'

The majority of the design is shared. 'I work more on the manufacturing side, most of our manufacturing is outsourced and we work with different workshops around the country.' He continues: 'Guro does more of the styling and then I say what's feasible, what's not feasible and how we can make it work with the manufacturers.'

So how do they do it?

First, Nigel and Guro decide what pieces of furniture they want to produce and then design them. They draw them with their computer-aided design programme. They work with several wood manufacturers, mainly based in Devon, who effectively take their designs and cut them out.

Nigel explains: 'I'll send the computer-aided designs to these manufacturers who will produce the samples or the prototypes of the products and ship them back up to London for us and then it goes from there, a bit of refinement until we've settled on final designs and then we'll put in a bulk order with them.'

They have a fantastic website which really sets the scene and style of the products. Nigel explains: 'We've just been selling online up to this point through our website and we sell through Etsy, which is like a marketplace online for craft goods.' They are hoping to offer their products to more stores and are busy meeting executives to this end. 'We've been in contact with some people in different countries as well like New Zealand and Australia.' They are starting to move into the wholesale area and have made a lot of progress for such a fledgling business.

Avelere is yet to make profits. Nigel explains: 'I'd say on this business we probably invest more in development at the moment but because it's under the same umbrella as the base shapers business the group as a whole still makes profit.' The base shapers have been fantastic for them from day one and continue to support the development of Avelere.

Nigel's view is, 'to be an entrepreneur you've got to be quite optimistic and look at the longer term'. He recalls: 'I studied Economics at school and took Economics a long way through university as well and something I always looked into for that was short-term gain versus long term gain.' He continues: 'And you look at different examples of companies who've taken a short term profit and suffered in the long run and I've always tried to say to myself, I've got to focus on the long game even though it's slightly detrimental in the short term.' This requires a lot of confidence and determination.

He would not consider working for somebody else now. 'I think I'd struggle to be honest. I've never been the best at following instructions as it is.' The business is a priority. 'I plan my social life around my work more so, but that's because I enjoy doing what I do.' He admits he did not have the same enthusiasm as an employee: 'When I used to do these internships in banks, by Sunday evening I'd be like, oh God, I've got to go to work on Monday. Whereas now I don't mind if I sit around on my Sunday evening and do some work and I'm not like dreading going to work on a Monday. I'm happy to work till 9, 10 in the evening and it doesn't really bother me.'

There is much discussion in the press and academia about succession in businesses and moves to the next generation. Perversely for Nigel, his mother ran a computer-training business and he has gone back to traditional furniture. He has put a new spin on a traditional type of business, so normally you'd expect the next generation to be more computer literate, so has he kind of flipped that? 'I'm not saying I'm not more computer literate.' He grins but he has a unique concept for someone so young. The furniture business is not one associated with young graduates.

He thinks back to his choices: 'Coming out of university, having done a Business degree, I was like, great, I can run a business.' He then realised, 'I can't do anything.' He was not qualified formally to run a business. 'So it was more experimentation, figuring out something that I felt like I could do well and something that effectively I could afford to do as well.'

Nigel and Guro started on a shoestring budget. 'Generally furniture manufacturing can be a pretty expensive thing to do unless you're handmaking everything yourself.' This meant they had to be creative. Nigel was smart. 'We looked at traditional manufacturing techniques and ways that these manufacturers were working and figured out these are concepts that are easy for them to do and they're happy to do and we can get them at the right price, so how can we use these to create something?' He worked with the industry, seeing what was viable and then ensuring he fitted into this. This innovative thinking won him an award.

He managed to get to the finals of the Shell LiveWIRE award scheme. 'I actually got introduced to Shell LiveWIRE through a couple of friends from university who have also started a business and they won one of the monthly awards in 2014. I saw that they'd won this award and I went out for a drink with them and had a chat about it and they're like, you should definitely look into it, apply for it.' And so he did but failed to win the first time round. Nigel and Guro persisted, realising that the award money would be welcome but more importantly, the advice and contacts would be invaluable so they put in another application and won.

Shell LiveWIRE got in touch with them and told them that all the monthly winners could go forward and they were invited to apply for Shell LiveWIRE Young Entrepreneur of the Year. They had to fill out another application and pitch the business. 'I was fortunate enough to get picked for the final eight in the country, which is really cool', Nigel explains proudly. They had to put a lot of effort into the process. 'We had to write out a full business plan and give some presentations. We were invited along to a day that was held at the Shell building in Waterloo where we did this pitch and we had a question and answer session about our business plan and that was judged.' Nigel enjoyed it. 'It was fun, I got to meet some interesting people and other young entrepreneurs from the awards scheme who I didn't know. Unfortunately we didn't win but we were in the final so I was happy.'

The Shell LiveWIRE experience was really beneficial. 'I think there's a lot of benefits to Shell LiveWIRE. One thing I value a lot is the blog they run; they have a lot of different entrepreneurs who post articles, and it's generally different advice about how they're doing with their businesses, things that they think other entrepreneurs should be considering.' Nigel explains: 'I find that a really valuable resource. The reason I find it valuable is not just to see advice from other people but when you're working on your own company, especially a small company you haven't got this vast network of people that you can turn to. So even if you have these different mentors you can go and meet, it's nice to have this other set of advice that you can turn to and you know the people are good people, they know what they're talking about.'

Other than the contacts at Shell LiveWIRE, Nigel confesses: 'I talk to my dad a lot.' He continues: 'He's never run his own business but he's worked; he's been an IT consultant for years and years and he always helps me with the business side of things and he comes up with a lot of good ideas which really help me out and if I just want to talk things through he's quite level-headed, so he definitely helps me.' Nigel talks to his friends who run small businesses as well. 'For example, the guys who told me about Shell LiveWIRE, I meet up with them every few months and talk to them quite a lot on the phone; they definitely help me out as well.' This network is very important, 'because we're kind of going through the same thing at the same time and one of us has always done something slightly different and we're like, is this the right way to do it?' Nigel finds his peers are the people he actually turns to rather than more experienced people. 'I don't know, maybe it's just because it's harder to get the time with an experienced entrepreneur.'

On being an entrepreneur? Nigel claims: 'It's addictive. I think my characteristics as an entrepreneur reflect my characteristics of me as a person.' He continues: 'I'm like the eternal optimist; it's pretty hard to get me down. I'm always looking at the positives in everything and that definitely helps out in an entrepreneurship environment.' You need to be persistent to be an entrepreneur, 'You're trying all these different things and probably 80 per cent of them don't work or something goes wrong with it; you're always being constantly let down. But if you keep this kind of optimism it always picks you back up and keeps you going.'

He is also open to learning. 'I really love to learn. You get lots of online courses you can do from different universities. I'm always trying to take a few of these every month to keep on learning, just because I think you've got to keep developing the mind. You can't just focus on the one thing you're doing; you need to keep learning about broader things as well. So that's something that I think really helps me with the entrepreneurship as well.' Nigel did an Open University online course recently about the strategy framework and they have tried to implement it. 'Guro and I have been talking about it and thinking about different problems and solutions for the business.' His other strength is 'generally just being driven and trying to put as much time into it and be as committed to it as I can'.

He is aware of his shortfalls too. 'I'm quite easily distracted ... and I'm always the one who's going, but we could do this, we could do that, let's try this, let's try that. Guro is a lot more focused than me; she's able to guide me and keep me on the straight and narrow focusing on the things which will take us forward quicker.' He confesses: 'I'm more of a big picture person, always looking around saying, oh, but there's a business there to do, there's a business there.' He appreciates he needs to hone in. 'So, yeah, a little more focus perhaps would do me good, but then equally perhaps it would shut down other sides of my personality that help me out so, I don't know.'

Nigel's top tip to others thinking about entrepreneurship would be 'just do it'. Even if you are a recent graduate and working, 'it's probably taking up a lot of your time and if you've got these ambitions elsewhere then you've just got to set aside a bit of time in your evenings, get up slightly earlier, don't go out partying so much and just take a little bit of time and try out your idea', he advises. For example, 'if you want to start a website just go online and start a website and you can find how to do basically anything on Google these days. If you need to learn, Google it and you'll find an answer or you'll find a course'. He affirms: 'The only way to actually go into starting a business is to start something and you'll start out and honestly you'll probably be terrible. My first businesses were awful and even now I look back at Avelere like a month ago or two months ago and I'm embarrassed looking back because I'm like, oh why, that was so bad, why were people buying from us anyway?'

Experience counts, 'and the more time you put into it the better it'll get and I think it is something that you can do alongside another job to begin with. I think that's how you've got to start'. In terms of finance: 'Even if you have to put a few hundred pounds out of your own pocket into it I think it's worth it, at least you'll learn something and you'll come out of it a better person even if you don't go on with this business next time maybe you'll come up with something else and you'll go into that instead. So, my advice would be just give it a shot, put some time into it.'

His future aspirations are for Avelere to continue to grow and they want to open up their own series of shops and have a global presence. For Nigel personally: 'I enjoy starting up different businesses and looking at different kinds of creative challenges basically and putting a new twist on an old problem.' He will definitely go on and start up something new in the future. 'There's always a different adventure whenever you start something, a different experience.'

For more information and to watch an interview with Nigel Westwood, please visit our companion website at www.he.palgrave.com/dhaliwal-millionaire.

Key learnings

- Choose your business partner wisely
- Cut costs where possible
- Pitch your business idea effectively
- Understand and work with suppliers
- Enter competitions
- Just do it – put time into your business to get it going
- Develop your network, but be discerning
- Learn and grow.

References

Enterprise Nation. (2014). *Home Business Report.* In Association with Direct Line Insurance, www.enterprisenation.com/homebusiness, <date accessed 6 November 2015>
Higher Education Statistics Agency – www.hesa.ac.uk

Resources

Avelere – www.avelere.com
Hallbookers – www.hallbookers.co.uk
Shell LiveWIRE – www.shell-livewire.org
Start Up Loans UK – www.startuploans.co.uk

7 Support for Young Entrepreneurs – Accelerators

At Global Entrepreneurship Week in November 2015 David Cameron, then UK Prime Minister, said: 'The future of our economy depends on a new generation of entrepreneurs coming up with ideas, resolving to make them a reality and having the vision to create wealth and jobs.' He added: 'But to make it happen we need a culture change in Britain – an injection of self-belief and dynamism to convince those who are dreaming about making it big to get out there and do.' Accelerators are one way forward.

What do accelerators do?

Universities and colleges are familiar with the incubator model, and now the accelerator models are in vogue. Accelerators provide the chosen graduate with some money to buy them time and space. They provide networks and these can be very powerful. If you are creating value then many people want to get involved. They open doors to customers and investors and provide mentorship and education.

The Sirius programme, run by UK Trade and Investment, was introduced to enable graduates from all over the world to set up a business in the UK and to support them in doing this. This was done in two ways: they looked at the international student market and those that were already at UK universities, and travelled the world looking for new graduates who had not been to the UK. The Sirius programme offers 12 months of support in the UK, provides monthly financial support to the entrepreneur and will also endorse a Tier 1 Entrepreneur Visa. The Tier 1 Graduate Entrepreneur visa is in place for overseas students who want to stay in the UK and develop a business idea. This was introduced after the strict visa guidelines which mean overseas students can no longer stay in the UK after their studies have been completed.

There are several schemes offering help to start-ups and new entrepreneurs such as the Global Entrepreneurs Programme, which helps companies set up in the UK, and Oxygen Accelerator, which is a 13-week mentor-led boot camp which culminates in you pitching to venture capitalists, angel investors and private equity groups (www.gov.uk).

Sirius aims to fill the gap after university, when graduates need some level of support. It places selected teams within an accelerator programme and part of that agenda is to encourage regional growth. To date, there have been 75 winning teams.

Accelerate Cambridge at the Judge Business School is an interesting model because the emphasis is on mentoring rather than funding. It provides mentoring and support throughout the whole region in and around Cambridge, the university and the Silicon Fen which is a cluster of high-tech businesses in the region.

The Entrepreneur First accelerator programme is a novel model where top technology graduates are helped to build start-ups together. They take people at the very early stages before they have a team or even a start-up idea and give them three months of unconditional support such as funding to survive, mentorship and other support. This is done on an individual basis and they are helped to build teams and develop ideas together. To date, 50 companies have been started. The first cohort are now worth around £100 million in total. They have raised around £20 million in venture capital funding which is phenomenal given that the founders are straight out of university with little experience. It teaches graduates to think big and gives them a peer group of like-minded people who are tech-friendly. Practically, they offer initial funding and mentorship from experienced entrepreneurs, as well as other benefits such as office space, access to legal and accounting support and access to a broad international network of investors.

According to Matt Clifford, Chief Executive of Entrepreneur First: 'We created Entrepreneur First because we believe that in the 21st century, technology entrepreneurship is going to be the career of choice for the most talented and ambitious individuals. We need new institutions to support that transition: we want Entrepreneur First to be the place where the world's best founders meet their teammates, advisors and investors. We're excited to see the impact the programme is having on its participants – and we're even more excited by the progress they're making. Companies like SpeakSet [the company featured in this chapter] are bringing real innovation to sectors that have sometimes been resistant to new technology and in the process they are helping their customers save huge amounts of money and time, as well as greatly improving patient experience.'

The accelerator route is an attractive one for smart, tech-savvy young entrepreneurs. They offer networking, mentoring and the ability to interact with your peers, and go further in adding value than incubators and shared workspaces. Accelerators focus the entrepreneur, as you have to work towards pitching to investors within a time frame.

The downside of accelerators is that they take a slice of equity, which is sometimes more expensive in terms of equity than you might get from a venture capitalist. They provide selected graduates with money, but they must give a stake of their company for this. You get around £20,000 for an 8 per cent stake in the company. The role this money plays is to buy space and time for the entrepreneurs so they can focus on their technology. They provide mentorship and education and another enormous benefit is the networks effect which is very powerful. You meet not only with your cohort but with previous cohorts, speakers and other stakeholders. People want to get involved if you are creating value. It opens doors to customers and suppliers – and investors. Accelerators work with young, smart people. Below is one young entrepreneur who fits that description.

Matt Simmonds – SpeakSet and the Entrepreneur First accelerator programme

Oxford-educated Matt Simmonds was 23 years old when he co-founded SpeakSet. Together with Adi Kasliwal and Ewan Marshall, Matt has transformed the way older people connect with technology. Tackling the issue of isolation head on, these young entrepreneurs have eased the fears of the elderly with their high-tech solutions. They are helping the elderly with an age-defying video calling system that connects them to the world. More importantly it connects them to their care providers, thus preventing unnecessary home visits and easing loneliness and isolation. The entrepreneurs developed the idea and technology through the Entrepreneur First accelerator programme which provided them with education, mentoring, networks and funding for a stake in their business.

Matt studied engineering at university and he first got an inkling that he wanted to start his own business when he did an internship at

McLaren. 'I was working with the Formula 1 team for a summer and for me, as an engineer, that was the coolest job in the world.' He really loved it but at the end of his eight weeks he thought: 'I'm still working for somebody else and I'm kind of restless; I thought the only way to solve it was to go and start something myself.'

Matt confesses: 'I did absolutely nothing entrepreneurial at university.' He did not join any entrepreneurship society or get involved with extra-curricular activities in that vein. Through the grapevine, he heard about a talk by Entrepreneur First. 'I just thought I'd go along to see what it was all about, and that was the only hour I'd spent thinking about entrepreneurship at university.'

The Entrepreneur First accelerator programme was looking for the best graduates. It is a competitive process as they want to get the right people, and then throw them together in teams and let them come up with a good business idea in a challenging but supportive environment.

'At that stage it was a two-way thing', Matt explains, 'They were looking for candidates, so they came to university to try and recruit and if we were interested we had to go through a selection process.' Matt was keen and, together with Adi, his best friend from university, 'we thought we'd have a crack at starting a business straight out of university', he explains.

Matt and Adi were selected to go on the Entrepreneur First accelerator programme. Matt explains: 'Entrepreneur First works differently to lots of other start-up accelerators. It's not interested in your idea or even your team. It just selects purely on the basis of individuals.' By that he means: 'It gets lots of smart graduates, puts them in a room and helps them form a business.' This is an innovative approach and Matt agrees: 'It is a very unusual way of doing things but it's been really successful.' The programme helped them to generate ideas, and 'we'd get various people from industry to come in and tell us about what they did, and we'd try to find problems that we could solve and build a business out of'. The programme also helped form teams. 'We went away together for two weeks to get to know each other and get in a different environment.' Following this they had mentorship programmes. 'We had some structure. Really the whole thing was about adding structure around starting a company.' Matt found the experience invaluable.

Matt and Adi met Ewan on the programme. 'We tried all sorts of different ideas from online dating to marketing to smart homes and failed abysmally at all of them', Matt confesses. They all came together, however, around the idea of building technology for older people. 'We did this because Ewan was actually living with his grandparents when he was on the programme and he saw problems every day with his elderly grandparents that he would solve using technology.' For example, they had never seen their great-grandchild because he lived in the south of France and they were housebound. 'They couldn't go and visit him, so obviously Ewan got on Skype and showed them their great grandchild.' Similarly, they had all sorts of problems around shopping and getting shopping delivered, so Ewan would solve that by online shopping. This led us to think that, 'actually building technology for older people would be a really good thing'. He continues: 'So we just set out basically to understand how we could help.' They conducted their market research thoroughly. 'We sat in care homes for about four or five months and just got to know lots of older people, really tried to understand their lives, what they did, what they were interested in and how we could help.' Through that process, 'we learnt that the biggest problem in old age is isolation'. This led them to their business idea. 'Building a system that connects older people to the rest of the world, through that you can do a lot of good.' Pressures on the health service coupled with an ever-growing ageing population mean that it's no wonder more people are worried about growing old. Costs of care homes are sky high. Receiving care in your own home offers so much more comfort, and staying connected with the outside world is healthier.

The result is SpeakSet, a simple video calling system that connects older people to their care providers, thus saving care providers time by preventing unnecessary home visits and making older people less lonely and less isolated by connecting them to the rest of the world.

'There's two sides to the system', Matt explains: 'There's the side that the older person uses, which is a really simple system that works through the television. It works through the television because this is the one piece of technology that pretty much everyone's familiar with, and through that system you can turn it on, you can place a call with one button and you can have a chat to anyone around the world. From a care provider's end, a GP, district nurse or a carer can just log in on their laptop and make calls through their laptop.'

The young entrepreneurs had found a sound business proposition and were working hard on developing it on the Entrepreneur First programme.

Officially the course ran for about six months, 'but the support never really stopped, we're still in touch', Matt explains. He adds proudly: 'Matt Clifford, who founded Entrepreneur First, sits on our advisory board, and we can always pick up the phone and talk to him. We're part of a community now.'

Group dynamics

As a group the young co-directors work well. 'It's all pretty even; the three of us make decisions as a whole.' Matt continues: 'Of course we're all putting everything into this. There's heated discussions, but I think we all fundamentally really respect each other, and that's really important.'

They have gained experience as entrepreneurs, and have spotted opportunities and identified a big gap in the market. Matt explains: 'Nobody so far has built good technology for older people and this is the demographic that needs technology the most.' They are at an advantage. 'I think we do that better than everybody else because we've actually sat down and listened to older people.'

There is an ageing population and Matt continues: 'There's a really big shift in the way that we deliver care, and that will continue to happen over the next 10, 20, 30 years, so we really want to be at the forefront of how care is delivered.' He feels strongly that, 'shifting care towards the home where people are most happy and being able to do things like remote video consultations, being able to monitor blood pressure, heart rates all from the comfort of your own home is really good for both carers and patients'.

Matt explains that SpeakSet sell directly to care providers: 'It's always free for the patient, and we sell to care providers because, care providers use SpeakSet because it saves them money and makes care easier to deliver.'

Matt and his team started SpeakSet because they passionately wanted to help elderly people. Ewan's grandparents had specific issues and the team wanted to use their know-how to create a technology to help them. Matt asserts: 'I think my advice to anyone starting a company is just do something that genuinely does some good.' He continues: 'It's so much easier to get things off the ground if you have people around.' He stresses: 'You need to build a support network, and if people around you think what you're doing is actually doing some good for society they will really rally behind you and help you.' He says proudly, 'that's been a really good thing about SpeakSet'.

Matt would not trade in his entrepreneur status for a safe job. 'I absolutely love what I do, and I wouldn't want to do anything else.' A lot of his friends 'have gone into City jobs and that kind of stuff. It's not really for me', he says. 'I think if I'm going to work really hard, then I think working hard for myself is a really good thing, and having the freedom to actually choose what I do every day is a really exciting thing.'

The business has clearly benefited from good mentors but how did they access finance? Matt explains: 'Early support is really important.' They have benefited from support from the Nominet Trust and through the Big Venture Challenge and Impact Hub as a series of grants. The grants they received, 'total up to about £120,000 over the course of probably 18 months', Matt explains, 'and then we raised another £295,000 in seed funding'. The business has been running for three years now and they are close to breaking even.

Looking at who influences Matt: 'I think definitely people who are now officially on our advisory board, but there's a few people, basically people who have been there and done it before and people who are really honest about how it went.' One of his role models is Nadav Rosenberg, 'who actually started Groupon in the UK'. He also sings the praises of Matt Clifford, who started Entrepreneur First. 'I think they're people we look up to because you can go to them with a problem, and it will feel really hazy and difficult, and they will just be able to cut through all of it and say this is what you're going through, I've seen it before.'

Summary

The organisations discussed here can offer hope and direction and can be life-changing for young entrepreneurs. You need to know exactly what is being offered and your responsibilities too. The support given is invaluable – money, networks, open doors, mentors – offering you a safe environment to thrive in. The following chapters look at more young entrepreneurs who have gone through these organisations.

For more information and to watch an interview with Matt Simmonds, please visit our companion website at www.he.palgrave.com/dhaliwal-millionaire.

Key learnings

- Start with a big problem
- Make the most of the accelerator experience
- Find the right team
- Do your market research thoroughly
- See how you can save organisations money
- Help others – do something that's good for society.

Resources

Entrepreneur First – www.joinef.com
Sirius Programme – www.gov.uk/government/collections/sirius-programme-for-graduate-entrepreneurs
RBS – www.inspiringenterprise.rbs.com
Shell LiveWIRE – www.shell-livewire.org
SpeakSet – www.speakset.com
Start Up Loans UK – www.startuploans.co.uk
The Bright Ideas Trust – www.brightideastrust.com
The Prince's Trust – www.princes-trust.org.uk

8 Where's the Money?

It's cool to be an entrepreneur but how can I afford it? The trouble with being young is that you have fewer savings. If you are at university or have just graduated you probably also have a lot of debt.

The first port of call for entrepreneurs is their own savings, what little they have, followed by help from family and other close relatives. Most start off with small or virtual businesses requiring less capital at the start-up stage. The most common means of funding start-ups is through bootstrapping, which is using the minimum amount of financial resources, thereby reducing risk. Bootstrapping is the byword for young entrepreneurs and it means doing things by yourself as cheaply as possible. Some young entrepreneurs have won seed funding at various competitions, for example at their university or with a bank, while others have secured funding from The Prince's Trust, Shell LiveWIRE or other organisations.

Crowdfunding is increasingly the way forward for young entrepreneurs, where they raise small amounts of money, often via websites, from many people. Some have access to angel investors who are wealthy private individuals who want to invest in entrepreneurial ventures for any number of reasons – friendship, altruism, a desire to support the entrepreneur or a belief in their product or service. They are hard to find so be nice to them.

But what else is out there?

The early stage in financing is informal investors and then banks until you go up the ladder to venture capitalists. As the business develops, finance comes from retained profits (Deakins and Freel, 2012).

According to Bygrave and Zacharakis (2014) self-funding by entrepreneurs, along with funding from informal investors, is the lifeblood of

an entrepreneurial society. Informal investors are close family and relatives, then friends, other relatives, work colleagues and business angels.
The rarest source of capital for new start-ups is venture capital. This tends
to be more for the larger biotechnology and nanotechnology companies
rather than smaller start-ups. The amount of capital that entrepreneurs
need to start their ventures depends on the type of business, the ambitions of the entrepreneur and the location of the business.

Some take an equity stake for lending money such as with the accelerator model we discussed in Chapter 7. The advantages of equity financing
are that if a business doesn't make a profit, the investor doesn't get paid,
and they cannot force the business to go bankrupt. Thus it is in the interest of the investor to see the business succeed, and so they are likely to
provide helpful advice and valuable contacts (Mariotti, 2014). The downside is that the entrepreneur loses some equity and thus some control
over the business and the investor is likely to want a say in how it is run.

Business incubators provide an affordable place for the business
and offer everything from office space to services, equipment, advisors
and potential investors, plus the ability to network with other similar
entrepreneurs.

In most cases you need a business plan to raise capital and to pitch
your business idea (Kirby, 2003; Southon and West, 2002; Burns, 2014). It
is important to have a solid rehearsed pitch, as you never know when you
will need to use it. An elevator pitch is a concise version of a pitch. Imagine you are going up an elevator with an important potential investor; you
only have three minutes to convince them of the viability of your business. There are some excellent examples of elevator pitches on YouTube
and the link to one of these is provided in the Resources section below.

There are myriad sources of support available for young entrepreneurs
but it's important for you to be discerning and see what really works
for you. The government has several initiatives to help young people to
set up their own businesses, including Start Up Loans UK who provide
advice, loans and mentoring. They have helped over 2000 young entrepreneurs but you do have to pay interest and pay the loan back.

Shell LiveWIRE Smarter Future Programme supports young, innovative entrepreneurs aged 16–30 who have traded for less than a year or
are about to start up in the next six months. It is aimed at those who
have an idea that addresses the UK's future transport, energy or natural
resource challenges, or makes our urban environments cleaner and more

sustainable places to live and work in. Start-up funding is £5,000 and is awarded to one winner per month. These winners are then eligible to be considered for the annual Shell LiveWIRE Young Entrepreneur of the Year award which is worth £25,000.

Another source of support is The Bright Ideas Trust, which was established in 2007 by Tim Campbell, winner of the first *The Apprentice* programme. It is a charity helping young people in London who are not in employment, education or training. They have helped thousands of young people to start up and run businesses by providing advice, guidance, mentoring and training.

The Prince's Trust is an established organisation, having been around for 30 years, and boasts a high-profile patron, Prince Charles. It is a tremendously helpful support organisation. They raise money from high net worth individuals, and this money comes from the Treasury. They focus on young people who are unemployed or struggling at school and aged between 13–30 years old, and help them with grants, programmes and mentoring. They aim to enhance skills in a useful, fun and interactive way. They have a vast network of supporters who help mentor young people and the trust has flourished over the years, producing some excellent sustainable businesses.

The Prince of Wales' charity has helped more than 825,000 young people since 1976 and supports over 100 more each day. The Prince's Trust offers financial help, legal advice, business support and mentoring. Martina Milburn, Chief Executive of The Prince's Trust, said: 'Our Enterprise programme has provided a lifeline to thousands of disadvantaged young people, helping them to get their lives on track and realise their potential as young entrepreneurs. In addition to creating a job for the entrepreneur, new businesses enrich their surrounding communities. It is critical we continue to nurture young people's passion for business and invest in the next generation.'

Here we look at two young entrepreneurs who turned to them and also turned their hobbies into businesses.

Demi Owoseje, Majeurs Chesterfield

Respect everything and waste nothing were values instilled in Demi Owoseje from an early age by her mother. These were to be the founding principles of her company Majeurs Chesterfield, which restores furniture.

The business was born out of frustration when she could not find a job after her studies and what started off as a hobby soon turned into a business with big plans. She turned to The Prince's Trust for help and enrolled on their entrepreneurship programme which gave Demi a mentor, funding and a vast network of contacts, enabling this dynamic woman to blossom in the business world.

Demi Owoseje is an accidental entrepreneur. The business was, 'an absolute mistake', Demi recalls ruefully. 'It was an accident, and by that I mean I simply started it as a hobby because I couldn't find work.' Demi was 24 years old when she completed her degree in architecture at London Metropolitan University and the workplace was not kind to her. She was increasingly frustrated. 'I was commuting to a job from London to Luton for about a year. I wasn't happy doing that', she explains. That job was with an architecture firm but given the difficulty of the commute she made the decision to find a job in London. This proved difficult. 'I didn't find work for the longest time, and I simply started restoring furniture as a hobby.' She soon realised that she could make a little bit of money from it and so carried on doing it. 'I thought, well, I need money, this is making money, why not stick to it? And that's what I did.'

Demi continued with the business from home for a further two years but it was proving difficult. 'Once I used up all the space at home I then transferred the stock to a small storage unit locally and then we were selling from there, as well.' She had also developed a website. She needed bigger premises and warmer ones, as the storage units were draughty. Demi approached The Prince's Trust who helped her with some funding to assist with the move. 'I think we got about £4,000, but it wasn't really about the money because we were making money already. We were already trading.' It was the professionalism the organisation gave her that she valued. 'For me, The Prince's Trust was really taking me from somebody who was basically winging it, because I knew nothing about what I was doing, to then refining my skills a little bit more and understanding what it actually took to run a business and to take a business from just a wheeler dealer, which is what I started off as, an eBay trader, to somebody who actually had premises, who was online, who had a company image, a logo, a real brand.'

They gave her the help, support and advice to professionalise the business. 'Well, they helped us to refine ourselves a little bit more', she declares, continuing: 'They provided the mentor, which was the key for me.' It's to her credit that Demi realised she was stuck. 'This is one of the reasons why I approached them in the first place.' She had got a recommendation about them from a friend, 'who had spoken quite highly of their mentor programme, and I thought I need a mentor'. She was not disappointed. 'They provided me with an amazing mentor and she basically was able to give me her know-how of the business world, of how she has run businesses in the past and helped me refine my skills to know what I'm doing and have a direction.'

Demi was pushed into entrepreneurship because she was unemployed, so she picked something she was good at and turned this hobby into a business, seeking help and advice to take it to the next level.

Her Nigerian-born parents are very proud of her. 'I think the proudest moment for them was meeting Prince Charles because my dad's called Charles and my mother's called Elizabeth, so you can imagine how weird that was. My father came to the UK in the sixties and my mother joined him later.' Demi has got her work ethic from her parents. 'They've worked incredibly hard and it's just something that we've been brought up with, I suppose, me and all my siblings.'

It was not easy though. 'I think for me it was just doubt.' Demi lacked confidence. 'A lot of it was, oh, can I really create a brand? can I really open up? create a website that's fabulous? can I really face customers and sell them my work? because really it was my work.' It was very personal; she was allowing the world to judge her talent. 'I was restoring these things by hand, and I was self-taught, so can I really learn something off YouTube, do it myself and then sell it to somebody and get money for it? No way!' Her biggest challenge was overcoming, as she puts it: '[that] self doubt of, oh, can I, can I, should I, should I, and I think just saying, OK, I'm scared but I'm going to do it, anyway, and then seeing how that translated into a real sell and progress, and that's what gave me the bit of confidence to just keep going and taking those baby steps, and I think that for me has probably been my biggest challenge, and it still is my challenge, because you have an idea in your mind, it's like, OK, I want to do this but can I really do it, and I suppose it's just working through the fear.'

Demi's customer base varies from individuals to business to business (B2B). 'We do a lot of C2B (customer to business). We do a lot of B2B business, as well. So it's an array of people.' What is certain is that she stresses: 'the most common denominator within our clientele is just that it happens to be a lot of creative people, people who are very aware of sustainable furniture or the environment or people who just literally want to save a bit of money but get some good-quality furniture.'

Her love of bargains and art have served her well. 'I've always had an eye for bargains, because even from a young age I've always shopped at little charity shops', and she credits her mum for this: 'She always wanted the best but didn't always have enough money to buy the best so she'll go to the charity shops or flea markets or antique markets, and then she'll always dig through all the rubbish to try and find that one beautiful piece or unique thing you can take home and be really proud of.' Demi's upbringing, which has taught her to appreciate the value of money, has held her in good stead. 'That's how I've grown up, to always save money and to always want quality but also be mindful that rubbish isn't necessarily rubbish; it just depends on your perspective of it.' This has been a powerful lesson for her business. She has a social conscience and is determined to lead an ethical business, which demonstrates responsibility; 'that is very important' she asserts.

In addition, Demi's study of architecture reinforced these values. 'My favourite type of architecture was sustainable architecture, making something from nothing and using local products and local materials ... I did a project in India that taught me how to use local resources to create something beautiful and I think that's what I've transferred into my business', she explains proudly. 'Restoration's a huge thing for us.' She continues: 'As much as we love new products and new, fresh furniture and homeware products, we also like to restore the old pieces and we like to merge that, because I think that's a beautiful thing to do, and if you can do that I think you have something incredibly unique in your products.'

This passion has enabled the business to flourish and Demi now employs three interns. 'We've gone up to at least five at times, and I'm always happy to take people on and pay them what I can, and if I can't pay them anything I can at least give them some work experience so that they can then go off with a little bit of a skill and then get further employment.'

Demi confesses, that growth can be, 'very frightening!' It is difficult when more money is going out than coming in, particularly as she has had to invest in her website and operations as well as stock. 'I think we've made a lot of mistakes', she confesses. 'Like most business people, I think there have been times when we've put money into the wrong things and we've not necessarily had a return on it.' This is frustrating. 'It's like you're pulling your hair out and like we have no money, why have we spent all this money on this and I think it's just a learning process.' Experience has to be gained. 'You just do it to try it, obviously not to an extreme, and then just play with what works and what doesn't work.' Demi remains pragmatic: 'There have been times when we've spent money and it's been fruitful, and there have been times when we've invested money and we've got nothing from it, and I don't really necessarily think that you can avoid that.' She always keeps an open mind: 'That's a learning curve that you just have to go through.'

Demi seems to go against the grain of the go-getting risk-taker. She appears to be somebody who's very sensible. Her mother has taught her certain values about saving money and she has developed her own principles about restoring things. So is she a risk-taker? 'I am quite a risk-taker in the sense that things that I'm scared of, I will throw myself into it and do it, teeth shaking, wobbling feet and knees, I will still do it, and I think in that sense I'm a risk-taker. But I think as a young businessperson, as a start-up business, you're quite limited. If I had millions in the bank I'd probably take a lot more risks, but I don't. So I think it's just about understanding your limitations and being quite brave within those limitations, and that's as much risk as I can really afford at this stage.'

Being young and being in business has its upside: you have more get up and go. 'I think it's just the energy and the tenacity, and that go-get attitude. That's almost like naïve characteristics in you, that you have an idea, we could just do it; there's nothing stopping us from doing it. As much as we're scared there's nothing stopping you from doing it; whereas somebody who's a lot more mature, who's experienced life a lot more, is almost quietened a little bit and you're more cautious. But as a young person who has no real responsibilities, and by that I mean children, a husband and all of that, I think I'm a lot more free, and I think that's definitely the benefit of being young and in business.'

Demi's biggest strength as an entrepreneur is her 'go-getting attitude'. 'I don't take no very easily.' She will persevere. 'If something is a no I'm probably going to want more and I probably will push for it a lot more. That's definitely my strength, because there's been times when doors have closed in my face but if you push a little bit harder you'll be surprised what doors you open.'

With respect to finance, at the beginning Demi made a little bit of money herself from her paid hobby and then The Prince's Trust gave her some money towards larger premises. The problem she finds is that access to finance is confusing. 'Finance providers could probably market themselves a little bit better, especially to young businesses, so that you know what's actually available to you, because I was in business for quite a long time before I knew about The Prince's Trust.' She knew they were there to support young people in difficult situations, but in terms of entrepreneurship and business, she confesses: 'I didn't know that connection was there.' She credits the government in their initiatives to help. 'I suppose in terms of getting finance, the government has done an awful lot to help young businesses like myself to get access to finance, but I think the marketing, there's something missing between, something not quite connecting between the two. Although there are loads of programmes out there, they could market it better, a lot more people [would] have access to it and I suppose you could do a lot more a lot quicker.' Better signposting is required.

Demi is getting ready to launch her new range of furniture. 'We're going to start designing hopefully towards the end of this year our own ranges, and just experimenting a lot more with our materials and our furniture, our designs, and leather in particular. That's what we'll be doing for the next year', she explains excitedly.

She turns to fellow business owners for help and support, as well as her mentor. 'I've joined a lot of networking things. I've even turned a few of my suppliers and manufacturers into mentors, because they have the know-how.' Her suppliers, 'have the experience that I need access to'. Talking to them is a shortcut. 'If I were to go through it myself it might take me a number of years to get to where they are, but if I just tap into what they've already done and what they're currently doing, it fast-tracks what I'm doing. So I tend to turn to a lot of my fellow business people that I deal with on a day-to-day basis and basically ask them to be my mentor. So I have a mentor for every area, really, and I think that's definitely something that I would encourage any businessperson to do. Why do it yourself when you can get somebody else who's done it and told you what not to do as opposed to what to do?'

Her advice to other people is: 'Do it, simply. There is no substitute for experience; you've got to just throw yourself into it, and sometimes you'll feel like you're drowning but you must call for help whenever you need it.' She continues: 'And don't be afraid to go to people. There are times when I've called absolute strangers that I've found online. I'll call companies and start asking questions, such as how long did it take you to set that up? What's your design process? When do you launch your marketing for a particular product that's coming out? There are things that I don't have the answers to, and Google does not have all the answers. Sometimes you just have to connect with people to ask them the questions you don't know the answers to, and you'll be surprised who would help you if you just ask for help. Don't hold back. Just do it.'

Demi says: 'What's the worst that can happen? You can't lose money that you don't have. Throw yourself into it. Try it. When something goes wrong take a step back, look at what happened but don't let that stop you from trying it again.'

Having gone from an unemployed young person to businesswoman in the space of four years, Demi has grown enormously in confidence and business acumen. 'I think it's definitely been a growth spurt for me. The person I was before had ideas but was a bit lost. I think I was a bit naïve as well because I thought I can do this, I can do that, I don't know how yet but I can figure it out. And I suppose now I'm transforming from somebody who was dreaming of ideas to somebody who's now actively seeking to bring about those ideas, and I think that's been the biggest transformation for me, that. And I'm learning every day that action, plus whatever idea you've conceived in your mind, is the key to getting things done. I'm educating myself in the world of business now on a day-to-day basis, reading lots of business books, going to lots of networking events, learning from other people.'

Demi started the business cautiously, turning it from a hobby to a profitable business. She developed her creativity and craft and then secured funding from The Prince's Trust, which gave her professional business advice, which was of almost more importance than the funding. Demi worked well with her mentor and took on board any feedback, thus developing her own potential and confidence as well as her focus on the business. The Prince's Trust was the right organisation for Demi, as she needed the wider help and support they could give her. It's really important that you know what your business needs before you decide where to get financial help.

For more information and to watch an interview with Demi Owoseje, please visit our companion website at www.he.palgrave.com/dhaliwal-millionaire.

Key learnings

- Turn your hobby into a business
- Utilise your resources wisely – waste nothing
- Professionalise your business
- Apply for funding then spend money wisely
- Have an ethical business.

Money is one resource, but you need other forms of support such as mentors, networks as well as bags of confidence. Next we will hear from another young entrepreneur who turned to The Prince's Trust for support in setting up her business. Gabrielle Evans runs a garden design and maintenance company operating throughout London and the UK.

Gabrielle Evans – Gabrielle Gardens

University graduate Gabrielle Evans started her business at the age of 28 off the back of the recession. Having been made redundant from her job in computing, she was keen to use her skills and time wisely and had toyed with the idea of running her own business. Taking on a part-time job in a plant nursery, she knew this was the opportunity she needed to put her business plan into action; she now had the time and space to do this. She took on some freelance work for designers and developers as a landscape architect, thus building up her contacts and knowledge base while at the same time becoming an expert on plants and gardens at the nursery. Defying the myth that gardeners are older, she launched her business Gabrielle Gardens, offering designs and gardening services. The business blossomed.

Gaby, as she likes to be called, had always known what she wanted to do; her family are in business and so it was only natural that Gaby would follow suit. 'My whole family run their own businesses in one way or another or they work as freelancers', Gaby explains. Her mother has been a big inspiration to her. 'My mum had an interior design business throughout the 1970s and 1980s. She emigrated from New York when she was 17 years old without knowing anyone and without any kind of experience, and she was lucky enough to build this career for herself in the UK, so she has quite an entrepreneurial spirit, and I think that's trickled down to all of us.' She continues: 'My dad, as well, he also had a film production company.' There is no such thing as sibling rivalry in the Evans household. 'My sister is also a garden designer, so we work together occasionally on projects.' Of her two other siblings she says: 'My brother also has his own film production company, and my other brother has his own property company.' They all seem to have been influenced by their mother and her positive spirit and admire her strong work ethic. 'I don't know if it makes a difference but, perhaps when you have come from another country and you come to a new place without any lead, she had to be quite entrepreneurial in her approach.'

Gaby went to university in the UK and in Sweden to study resistant materials – wood and metal craft – which was intrinsic to where she is now. 'Being abroad, I think, was really important for my personal development.'

She started her business, 'really off the back of the recession, the Lehman Brothers recession', she recalls. 'I was made redundant from my job as a computer-aided design (CAD) technician. At the time I was working for an interior design company.' She continues: 'I was unemployed for about a year and then I got a part-time job working at a plant nursery and then I started to do some freelance CAD work for a variety of different property developers and interior designers and stuff like that, and then I got a CAD, a freelance CAD job for a landscape architect, so I started to do some landscaping CAD work.'

Meanwhile Gaby was gaining all of this horticultural experience from working part-time at a local plant nursery on minimum wage. Having made up her mind to start her own business, her first steps were to market her services. 'I really just went out there, got some flyers made and just started to flyer west London like there was no tomorrow for garden maintenance services, because I was quite desperate at that point to make ends meet.'

Gaby was living in London where the cost of living is the highest in the UK. 'So I really just started to go out there, to the point where I was getting jobs quite quickly and I had to really step up my knowledge; it was a real steep learning curve for me but it catapulted me into progressing quite quickly.'

Gaby realised she needed help. She turned to The Prince's Trust for some financial help. 'I needed to buy some equipment and some tools just to start off, and I also just wanted to take a step back from what I was doing, to look at the business plan and really put that time aside to building a very realistic business plan for the next three years.' She was given a small loan by The Prince's Trust. 'It wasn't much', she explains. 'It was about £1,500, something like that, a small amount but it was enough to just get me started.'

More important than the money she found them really helpful in all sorts of ways; they helped her to reflect on all areas of her business and helped her to plan, reflect and move forward. Eager to get more business-savvy, she joined the enterprise programme, which was a weeklong programme where they went through the business plan. 'We looked at things like tax and VAT (value added tax)', she explains. 'We met with other entrepreneurs and just talked about businesses, and that was quite an inspirational time. You can sometimes feel quite isolated when you're starting your own business because it really comes off the back of that individual wanting to succeed, but that can be quite a lonely process.' She found the group camaraderie uplifting. The Prince's Trust also provided her with a mentor, whom she states, 'I still have to this day'.

'I started out just on my own with this garden maintenance business. I was initially just doing maintenance, mowing lawns and a bit of planting.' All Gaby had was a ladder and a car. Dispelling the myth that enterprise is opulent she claims: 'There's absolutely nothing glamorous about what I was doing, what I still do today.' Her services were in demand however. 'Eventually the diary started to get quite busy.' Her next step was to employ someone part-time, and now she has a team of two full-time members of staff and a part-time member of staff for the design work. 'We now have about 80 to 100 clients, so we run quite a busy garden maintenance operation', she explains proudly, 'and then we have on average between 10 and 15 garden design jobs a year, from complete rebuilds to reworking small areas of gardens to styling projects, and so it's quite diverse.'

It is a labour-intensive, hands-on business so how does she price her work? 'We price our job on labour and then we also operate a mark-up with goods and products and plants. We also charge a design fee for computer-aided design, and then for large projects or long projects we take a percentage of the overall billed cost', Demi explains.

The biggest challenge is pricing. Gaby admits: 'Because as someone who came into this industry sideways from another industry I haven't got any formal qualifications in garden design, so for me it was a real confidence thing for myself.' She finds it challenging to price correctly but has built up her confidence through experience. It has developed through her getting the coveted official stamp of approval from the Royal Horticultural Society. She was awarded a gold medal by them. 'So now I've really just started to price for my worth, but I think that was really the challenge.' She ponders why: 'I don't know if it's solely something that women struggle with and whether men also struggle with this, but it was having the confidence to think, yeah, I'm worth that. That was the struggle.'

Gaby's business is seasonal. 'During the winter we really lean on our design arm because we cease garden maintenance for a month in January.' This time is used to focus more on their garden design work and also to develop their strategy for the following season. It enables them to focus on marketing, PR and all the other elements of the business that they do not have time for during their busier periods. 'We're not big enough yet to have someone looking at that side of things all of the time, so actually January is a really good time to lay out what we're going to be doing the following season.'

Gaby's major strengths as an entrepreneur are her grit and determination. 'I think the more that someone says I can't do something and the more of a challenge that I'm faced with, the more hungry I am to succeed.' She continues: 'I'm not sure if that's a skill but that's something that really drives me, and I want to push through and give my absolute best in everything that I do.' She has a greater degree of self-confidence now as a businesswoman. 'I think having an ability to see in a 3D way and as a designer this is something that I've always had since I was born. I've always been quite artistic, so I think that's probably just a natural skill that's important.'

Her advice to young people going into business is 'to really work hard, and really push through the first couple of years because they're the hardest, because you're constantly knocked back. You feel out of your depth.' She admits: 'For quite a long time I don't know if anyone really fully gets to grips with feeling confident about where they are in the world, but particularly in those first few years it's about really pushing through even when times are tough and just remembering that these failures exist to help you learn and progress.'

We normally associate the garden maintenance business with middle-aged or older people. Gaby was in her twenties when she started and had to compete with more mature gardeners. She explains: 'In horticulture there is definitely a trend of older people being interested in plants and gardens and landscapes. It's often a second career for a lot of people.' However, being younger was never really an issue. 'I think actually it worked quite well to my advantage. And actually when I started competing at the flower shows, doing show gardens, I was always the youngest person, so actually to get a gold medal in your early thirties is quite an unusual place to be.' She continues: 'A lot of people are doing these flower shows when they're much older, like in their forties, fifties, sixties, seventies, even'. She found, 'being a young person in horticulture has its benefits', however, she concedes, 'except that you are quite isolated. It's not a very glamorous subject, so you don't have a lot of young people, people of your age around you, but the small percentage of young people that are into horticulture is lovely because we have actually a real network of people now. I know everyone in the RHS that are around my age so actually that's a real benefit.'

Gaby has turned a modest business into a stable one, and has developed the business taking on new clients and staff and growing in confidence herself. She has now expanded the business and benefited from her computer-assisted designs, as well as the hands-on side of the business. The Prince's Trust helped her to secure funding to buy the necessary equipment, but a small business must always be careful not to waste time or money. Given the seasonal nature of the business, Gaby makes good use of the quiet months to reflect and develop the business and to plan for the year ahead. Young entrepreneurs must reflect on their businesses often and plan carefully.

Summary

Both Demi and Gaby have grown enormously in terms of confidence and business acumen and both were helped by The Prince's Trust. The businesses are in different sectors but the skills required to make a business succeed are similar. They both need to approach their businesses in a professional way and learn about marketing, networking and financials, and they both benefited from good mentors. The money they received was small and thus they had to concentrate their efforts and spend it wisely. It's important to price your products and services correctly, and this is as much about confidence as it is about business. Provide excellent service, care about what you offer and be the best you can be.

Access to funds is the one of the most important aspects of a new business, and the type of business you have dictates how much you need and the best source for this. Being frugal is important, but look at all your resources, not just financial ones. A good mentor, for example, can save you time and money. Young entrepreneurs need to be creative with the way they raise money and the way they invest it.

For more information and to watch an interview with Gabrielle Evans, please visit our companion website at www.he.palgrave.com/dhaliwal-millionaire.

Key learnings

- Use your skills creatively
- Become an expert
- Plan, reflect and move forward with your business
- Know your industry and market
- Hire people cautiously.

References

Burns, P. (2014). *New venture creation: a framework for entrepreneurial start-ups*, Palgrave Macmillan.
Bygrave, W. D. and A. Zacharakis (2014). *Entrepreneurship*, 3rd edition, Wiley.
Deakins, D. and M. Freel (2012). *Entrepreneurship and small firms*. McGraw Hill.
Kirby, D. (2003). *Entrepreneurship*. McGraw Hill.
Mariotti, S. (2014). *The young entrepreneur's guide to starting and running a business*. Crown Business Publishing.
Southon, M. and C. West (2002). *The beermat entrepreneur*. Pearson. Prentice Hall.

Resources

Elevator Pitch – https://www.youtube.com/watch?v=Tq0tan49rmc
Gabrielle Gardens – www.gabriellegardens.com
Global Enterpreneurship Monitor – www.gemconsortium.org
Majeurs Chesterfield – www.majeurschesterfield.co.uk
The Prince's Trust – www.princes-trust.org.uk

9 Social Media and Technology

Apps are all the rage today and social media is a part of our staple diet. Billions of people worldwide have smartphones and several other technological gadgets. Adoption rates are so high, supply can barely keep up with demand.

Many sites are now household names, such as Pinterest, Facebook, Google Plus, Reddit, LinkedIn, Twitter and Snapchat and they are all interactive, with you at the centre as a big part of the story. There are discussion boards, groups, likes, dislikes and so on. Social media is a part of our lives and it is invaluable for business. According to Jagongo and Kinyua (2013) social media enables businesses to 'increase their worthiness, cultivate strategic partnerships and increase their contacts with customers and suppliers'. In addition, geographical barriers can be broken down. Social media allows businesses to 'communicate speedily and cheaply with customers as well as allow them to construct a database that can be used to generate business leads'. The benefits of social media include increased brand recognition, improved brand loyalty, more opportunities to convert and lower marketing costs, as well as richer customer experiences and insights.

You can now connect to your customers, suppliers and financiers more closely and really get to know them. This enables you, as a business, to respond rapidly to their needs, demands, complaints and praise. For many businesses today, online customers are as important, if not more so, than face-to-face customers (Harrah, 2012). Therefore you need to make an effort to network and to reach your customers and keep your web content fresh and appealing. You need to give a high quality of service, only much quicker than before. In this new age of instant gratification, consumers are demanding – and fickle.

This high web presence means your business network must be strong. After all, your website is your calling card; it has to be clear, up to date and high up on the internet rankings. Blogs, podcasts and links to other sites all build your reputation as an expert. Social networking builds brand and customer loyalty and is essential to business success.

All this requires thought and effort on the part of a young entrepreneur. So while it is easy to set up an online business, a successful one needs a lot of smart thinking and planning. There are so many new ventures appearing all the time; you need to stand out from the crowd. Below, one young entrepreneur with an innovative idea shares his story.

Amit Pate – Snaptivity

Inspiration comes from the strangest of events. It was to be the gruesome terrorist attack at the Boston Marathon that was the backdrop of an innovative new idea for Indian-born entrepreneur Amit Pate who at 24 encapsulated the dreams of many international students. Armed with a bachelor's degree from India, Amit came to the UK to study for a Masters degree at the University of Sussex where, together with a friend, they won a start-up competition for their initial business idea of anti-counterfeiting technology. Keen to explore this idea further, he was devastated when visa rules forced him to return to India before realising this dream. Persistence and perseverance paid off as he won a coveted place on the UK Sirius programme, beating off tough worldwide competition. The Boston bombings were a turning point as he was convinced his technology could have helped to identify the terrorists. Forming a strong team, he came up with Snaptivity; developed from cutting-edge technologies it takes the whole notion of photographs to a new level, enabling you to find yourself in photos no matter who takes them, when or where.

Destined to be an innovator, Amit was fascinated by trying new things and starting something of his own. He wanted to make a change that would help society – something creative. Amit grew up in a small town near Mumbai, where his father has a business manufacturing agricultural fertilisers. Amit watched his father go through tough times in his own business. 'There was a lot to learn growing up', he recalls, but adds warmly: 'My father has always been my inspiration'. And it was his father who Amit has turned to at every step of his own entrepreneurial journey.

Amit completed his bachelor's degree in India and then came to England to study for a Masters in Information Technology with Business Management at the University of Sussex. Always innovative, Amit had been brainstorming business ideas and was hooked on a new anti-counterfeiting technology that he was convinced could solve a major international problem. It was during this time that he met classmate Phong Vu, who was later to be a co-founder of Snaptivity. 'I met Phong at a café near the beach and we discussed the idea in detail', Amit recalls. 'Phong was excited about it and we started working together that very evening.' Amit then came across a competition at the university just a week later and submitted their idea, showcasing an early prototype. It was to be the start of something big.

'We won an award at the university's entrepreneurship programme called Startup Sussex', Amit recalls proudly. They started to develop the idea but due to visa restrictions he had to return to India. He was upset and frustrated but made the best of the situation, and with a Masters degree behind him he worked in several consulting jobs for locational web companies building up their technologies. He was astute and keen to learn about new technologies and how he could exploit them later on. Amit recalls: 'I was learning new things and exploring how I could benefit from these technologies as well.'

Amit was exploring lots of opportunities and programmes around entrepreneurship and came across one in Kochi, South India, called Startup Village. Amit attended a 15-day programme to get to know the start-up eco-system in India. 'I met interesting people but not passionate entrepreneurs', he recalls sadly. 'People came to the Startup Village looking for new career opportunities because they did not like their current job or boss at the multinationals they worked in.' Amit wanted more. He still hankered after his business idea in the UK.

He then found out about the newly launched Sirius programme in the UK and applied with his idea of an anti-counterfeiting technology.

Amit Pate with Phong Vu beat worldwide competition to win the UK's first-ever Sirius start-up competition with their innovative anti-counterfeiting technology. They beat over 160 aspiring entrepreneurs from over 30 countries to gain a place on the UK Trade and Investment (UKTI)'s new Sirius programme, which is designed for graduates with innovative start-up ideas who want to make the UK their home. It aims to attract talented entrepreneurs and the process is rigorous. Amit recalls making several pitches to experts from all over the world. He joined six other international teams and the aim for these businesses was to create new jobs, wealth and attract foreign investment. They would also benefit from access to 500 million potential customers in Europe.

Amit's business idea was particularly attractive because, according to the International Chamber of Commerce, counterfeiting costs the world over $600 billion. This fraud needed to be tackled and his business would provide consumers with the ability to check instantly whether their branded product was genuine or not using mobile phones.

Amit got his coveted visa to come to the UK. In addition, he received start-up support, which included a 12-month place on the accelerator programme. This offered him world-class strategic support, which was a combination of mentoring, help to gain clients for the business and support to develop the technology. He also received £12,000 of financial support for the year for his living expenses. 'It was a dream come true', Amit recalls.

Amit found the Sirius programme really helpful. 'I was put into an Oxygen Accelerator and we had lots of mentoring around how the business has to be grown.' An Oxygen Accelerator Amit explains, 'breathes life into high-tech start-ups and nurtures the entrepreneurs. It teaches them about business, lots of new technologies and gives real time feedback.' Amit explains: 'The feedback is crucial for a business at the early stage, and lots of mentoring helps.'

At the end of the accelerator programme they had a 'demo' day where they showcased their product to investors, potential clients and partners. It was a steep learning curve and it really developed Amit and got him thinking. More importantly for Amit, he was in the UK working on a business idea he was convinced would work. It was during the Sirius programme that the new and diverse team emerged. Belarusian Volha Paulovich joined Amit and Vietnamese Phong Vu.

After a couple of months on the Sirius programme Amit explains: 'We were working on the anti-counterfeiting technology which was about empowering consumers to identify whether a product is genuine or a fake.' This was, however, presenting problems for the founders and was too big a project for them to deal with as a start-up and it would have taken them too long to get it to the market. They were out of their depth.

Amit was frustrated; he knew he had something good with the technology but they simply did not have the time or resources to carry it through. Amit was looking for ideas.

Inspiration can come from the strangest of events. The horrific Boston bombings were to be the backdrop of an innovative new idea. The idea of Snaptivity came to Amit when he was watching a news channel about the Boston Marathon in the US. 'There was bombing at the Boston Marathon and the police asked people to submit their photographs to identify where the terrorists were and how they came into the crowd.' Amit recalls: 'People submitted millions of photos and it took them four to six months to actually identify some relevant photos.' Amit was convinced that with their technology, it would have taken just a matter of seconds.

'We then pivoted a little bit into this technology', Amit explains. By 'pivoting' he means they shifted their focus a little. They created Snaptivity, which uses the same anti-counterfeiting technology, but takes it in a different direction. 'Snaptivity is a product that helps one discover oneself in photos no matter who takes your photo, whether it's your friend or a stranger. If you're in the picture you get your snap. That's Snaptivity.' They have developed it using cutting-edge technologies such as location-aware and mobile sensors. 'The app is a completely free app; it's freemium.' They generate revenue through advertisements and cross-promotions.

The technology is very simple to use. 'You download the app and you enjoy travelling around. If someone takes a photograph of you, or of someone or something else but you are in the picture, you get an instant notification on your phone saying that someone has taken a photo of you and you can see it.' Amit continues: 'We cross match the mobile sensor data and using the match data we identify that you are in the picture without using face recognition. And that's how we protect users' privacy as well.'

Today Snaptivity has over 5,000 users and this number is growing fast. Snaptivity is partnering with events organisers and are expanding into the events space and stadiums. 'We will be in more than 15 countries and stadiums', Amit explains. They are looking for football and cricket stadiums to expand the business.

Amit explains: 'If Snaptivity had existed during the Boston marathon, the police would have found their job a lot easier because it's crowd sourced information gathering.' He continues: 'It would work really well at parties. I go to lots of university fresher parties, and we meet new friends and they tell you their names; in the morning you forget who you met', says Amit. 'This application helps you connect with the people who are in the pictures.' It will solve the problem of putting a name to a face.

Amit is proud of his co-founders and they each have their role and expertise. Phong studied a Masters in IT with Business and Management at the University of Sussex with Amit and has extensive experience in information technology and system architecture, having worked previously with IBM. He heads the technical integration team at Snaptivity and works on product development.

They were joined by Volha Paulovich, who worked in the events and advertising industry and is multilingual, speaking fluent Russian, Belarusian, German and English. She has a Bachelors in Marketing and E-commerce and heads the Marketing division at Snaptivity. They all hold equal status and rank within the business. 'We live together in a house in Birmingham and work on building this technology', Amit explains.

They operate a secular business model. 'We don't have any titles in our business; they are only for external use.' Amit is happy living and working together. 'We have lots of meetings; we have a daily, early morning meeting where we argue a lot. Then it's all about the business so whatever is good for the business we go with it. That's how the decision goes.'

They still have much work to do. 'Since it's a start-up, it's too expensive to get a patent on it, but we have a technology which is completely unique and different so we have all our algorithms on our servers, so it's protected in that way.'

No business is without its challenges. 'The greatest challenge has been meeting the expectations of people', Amit admits ruefully, referring to consumers and other stakeholders. 'When you bring your product to the market, the expectations of people keep rising and you have to meet those and there are tight deadlines.' He reminisces about the earlier days when he had all the time and space to 'build something and then break it and rebuild', but, 'when you enter into business there's a strict timeline and those milestones are a challenge'.

Amit is resolute though: 'Our ambition and vision is to bring a technology that helps people and has an impact on society. And that's how we want to grow.' He is not concerned with just growing the business in terms of revenue but on the impact it has on society.

They are careful to run an ethical business. 'Privacy has always been our main concern', and so they have built their product, taking account of this. 'We build our technology so that your privacy is not invaded and our technology helps you identify your own photos; it's not about someone identifying you in the picture.' They don't do any face recognition and they do not have any database of information about their customers. 'It's all anonymous', he confirms.

Apart from the technology, developing a business is challenging, particularly when it comes to financing it. 'Accessing finance is really difficult',

Amit concedes. Is it luck or judgement that plays a role in entrepreneurial success stories? 'We were lucky enough because of our idea. We got onto the Sirius programme; before that we received funds from Sussex University.' The actual start of their journey was via awards and competitions, 'that's how we got lots of clients and funding', explains Amit. More recently, they won an award from Microsoft's BizSpark valued at $60,000 to build their infrastructure. 'Our infrastructure cost is almost zero now', explains Amit.

There is no stopping this dynamo. 'We're trying to build a technology that's a base core line technology that goes into any of the camera applications.' Core line technology is the key technology components used in a product and are vital for the product to work. Amit is thinking about the big picture: 'Our next project is stadiums. Stadiums have spider cameras and they usually take pictures of the fans and when you see yourself on the big screen you wave your hands but you never get this picture because it's about ten seconds of the whole match on television. We want to make it more interactive; using our technology we can have a bookmark where it tells what time you were in the picture and you can even receive the picture on your phone. You can even play with the spider cameras; if the spider cameras stop on you then in the next ten seconds it will be panning you. We want to create a more engaging and interactive fan base.'

Despite their success and the fact that the three of them live and work together, they still need help, support and advice from others. 'We have an accelerator database where, if we have any trouble or if we need some help, we approach them; they are the first point of contact.' Then there's the Sirius programme: 'There are lots of UKTI members who really help', says Amit. 'We have gained lots of business connections from there that help us make more connections and share their experiences. And, of course, my dad.'

So, does Amit regret not being a salary slave like many of his contemporaries? 'I made my decision because I liked entrepreneurship and I wanted to start something of my own and create a change', he asserts. He admits he is too restless to take on a nine-to-five job; he finds it impossible to sit back and relax. 'That's not something I enjoy doing.' He enjoys working around the clock and while still in his twenties, he has the drive and energy to do this. The merits of being young and in business are that, 'you have less risk maybe, and there's no fear of failure, so you can fail ... a lot!'

Amit urges young people thinking about entrepreneurship to go for it: 'There's always a gap for improvement and if you can dream it you can build it, so don't stop, just go for it!'

Summary

Amit illustrates the dynamism and energy it requires to head up a new technology business. The demands to get it to market are tremendous in this fast-paced world. Young entrepreneurs thinking about high-tech ideas need to either find a gap in the market or take an idea forward. It may be that, like Amit, you have to change direction slightly as your original idea may be too big for you. Patience, innovative thinking and surrounding yourself with good people will take you a long way.

For more information and to watch an interview with Amit Pate, please visit our companion website at www.he.palgrave.com/dhaliwal-millionaire.

Key learnings

- Learn while you work for others
- Be alert to opportunities
- Get inspiration from daily events
- Innovate and exploit your opportunities
- Respect your team
- Persevere.

References

Harrah, R. (2012). 'Social media opens doors for young entrepreneurs', *Diversity Journal*, 6 November, http://diversityjournal.com/pdjnew/social-media-opens-doors-for-young-entrepreneurs/, date accessed 16 June 2015.

Jagongo, A. and C. Kinyua (2013). The social media and entrepreneurship growth: a new business communication paradigm among SMEs in Nairobi', *International Journal of Humanities and Social Science*, vol. 3, no. 10 [Special Issue: May 2013], pp. 213–27, http://ir-library.ku.ac.ke/handle/123456789/6930

Resources

Sirius programme – www.gov.uk/government/collections/sirius-programme-for-graduate-entrepreneurs

Snaptivity – www.snaptivityapp.com

10 High-Tech Entrepreneurs

As new technologies develop ever faster, it's even more important now to make things happen and not just wait for them. You must create opportunities, not wait for opportunity to come to you. It's important to see what doesn't work, what's going wrong and then think of ways to fix the problem.

Young entrepreneurs today are lucky they grew up with new technologies and social media. This benefits their businesses and is central to a lot of start-ups headed by young entrepreneurs. They have grown up in the web era and it's second nature to them.

The *Financial Times* (2015) highlighted Europe's top 50 tech entrepreneurs, and the businesses included music streaming, digital mapping and wearable devices. At the top of the list was Spotify founder Daniel Ek whose music streaming business is used by over 60 million people. Music lover Ek has been creating Internet websites since he was 14 years old.

In this fast-paced world, new technology is ever faster and young guns need to come up with new, innovative ideas to stay ahead of the game.

Charlie Davies is one such young entrepreneur who attempts to do just this.

Charlie Davies – iGeolise

Dynamic and charismatic, Charlie Davies has all the makings of a fledgling millionaire. He started his business activities before he was a teenager and has continued to match his passion for information technology with his love of people. Always trying to find a gap and helping where he can, Charlie has built his business iGeolise into a credible venture with his business partner Peter Lilley. Boasting some prestigious clients including Zoopla and Countrywide, the large property portals, iGeolise is a high-tech innovative company that focuses on time, not distance, to a destination. On the brink of hitting the big time, Charlie shares his journey.

An early developer, Charlie had his own business at the age of 12 fixing computers and designing websites for other people, mainly family and friends who couldn't understand the technology. He used his bicycle to get around and put his knowledge to good use. Charlie's commercial sense and spotting gaps in the market have been the backbone of his success. 'I was well paid', he claims, 'and I offered a really useful service'. He continued his web development and consultancy 'businesses' throughout his school years.

Despite coming from a professional family Charlie showed an early promise to be entrepreneurial. Charlie's father is a GP and head partner in a surgery so whilst he is an entrepreneur in his own right the family did not talk business much at home. His father is 'calm and calculated ... in a nice way', explains Charlie. Charlie's mother is a nurse and he also has three sisters and a brother who have all gone into the professions, mainly medicine and law. So this was quite a professional household for this fledgling dynamo.

For Charlie, despite his professional role models, information technology (IT) was his big passion. He got his first computer at the age of seven years old and he loved playing with it. He was fascinated with the way it worked, often taking it apart and then rebuilding it. He was curious.

With an emotional intelligence beyond his years Charlie seeks to understand people and then help them. Thus his passion for IT and love of people have been the formula for his success. He is a social animal, not afraid of approaching people, and has built up his networks. These qualities have held him in good stead.

Luck and chance coupled with confidence and ability play a huge role. It was his second job that was to prove his most significant and it was for a local television channel. His early promise showed as he got the job because the chairman had spotted him at a school performance and had been impressed. More importantly, it was while working here, at the age of 16, that he met Peter Lilley, who was later to become his partner and co-founder in iGeolise.

Charlie took a break from his entrepreneurial endeavours for a while when he went to study at Cardiff University graduating with a degree in Politics and Philosophy at the age of 22.

Partners

Charlie explains how his partnership with Peter Lilley developed. Charlie and Peter met when he was 16; they were both working at a local television channel and they were helping to raise money for parish councils. So perhaps it was divine intervention!

Both were frustrated at the way the company was run. Charlie recalls: 'I figured out how not to run a company. They screwed up and I learnt a lot more by seeing the company fail than I ever would have had it been successful.'

They stayed in touch while Charlie went to university and later set up iGeolise.

Age is but a number and the extraordinary pairing of the then 26-year-old Charlie with 54-year-old Peter Lilley raised eyebrows. There is an assumption that it is a mentor-type relationship. However, that is incorrect; despite the 28-year age difference they are equal partners carrying equal responsibility both financially and operationally.

Charlie had always wanted to run a business and his early success strengthened this resolve. His drive, however, was not the lure of the possibility of limitless earning potential, nor the desire to escape being a salary slave. He desired to build something that people use and get benefits from. He wanted to help people, solve their problems and make life easier for them. From the age of 12 when he first rode his bike to his customers, it was his desire to provide a useful service that drove him.

Charlie is now the director and co-founder of iGeolise, heading up the product and technical side of the business. iGeolise have developed websites and apps that look at the time it takes to travel, rather than the distance. Charlie explains: 'What we have essentially done is invent a way that we can search maps by time instead of distance.' Currently, most online location-based searches are done by distance, for example a search may tell you a certain road is 10 miles away. Charlie continues: 'The big problem with that is that people don't tend to travel in a straight line, they are at the mercy of the transport networks around them.' Their technology enables users to find the quickest way to a destination. This has tripled the conversion rates for his big business clients which include Zoopla and Countrywide, Jobsite and Visit Britain. They have also worked with *The Guardian* and TalkTalk, and there are several others companies in the pipeline.

Humble beginnings

In the early days Charlie worked in his parents' loft but the business needed a more professional space in order to meet clients and conduct day-to-day business. Having a strong network is essential for any entrepreneur and Peter knew one of the senior managers at the University of Surrey and had heard about SETsquared. SETsquared is an incubator set up to help technology companies. It is a collaboration between the universities of Bath, Bristol, Exeter, Southampton and Surrey and it supports high-tech start-up companies. Its mission is: 'To help turn an innovative spark into a thriving, commercial business.' (setsquared.co.uk). Practically, they offer office space and facilities as well as access to industry specialists, investors and business mentors.

The business moved to SETsquared, part of the research park at the University of Surrey. This incubation programme provided iGeolise with a more professional environment where the offices are fully manned so the entrepreneurs can focus fully on developing the business.

Starting a business can be a lonely process, especially at the outset, and SETsquared opened up the ability to network with other businesses. This was more stimulating for Charlie who had been stuck in his parents' loft. It also had the advantage of allowing them to meet other early-stage entrepreneurs who were committed to growth, as they all had to pass a screening process to get in.

Charlie enthuses: 'SETsquared was fantastic.' He continues: 'It's there to essentially help technology companies primarily to kick-start their business. So there's lots of things that you don't really think about for businesses but people need somewhere to sit, they need Internet access, they need meeting rooms, they sometimes need the bravado of looking much bigger than they actually are, especially when it comes down to your first sales and trying to establish yourself as a name.'

This move really helped the business: 'What a lot of incubators like that do, and SETsquared do it particularly well is provide you with everything that you need to do and use.' Their company benefited from shared services such as access to accountants, lawyers, potential PR, training and recruitment. This meant they could focus on the things that make their business unique and not waste time and effort having to worry about all the other things.

What was important to Charlie was that the premises were heavily subsidised. 'I spent an awfully long time living in my parents' loft in a small room and working and sleeping within three feet of each other. It was good to go to the office and call myself a working person.'

The start-up phase of a business can be challenging and inexperienced Charlie felt the pressure and had some doubts. It was all getting to him: 'It's just an impossible scenario. I sometimes think I almost did it the wrong way round. I didn't go into industry at all, so I've pretty much always made my own money, either doing odd jobs or when I was younger fixing computers; I'd never really had any contacts.' He was conscious that his business contacts were limited and had to make great efforts to get up to speed.

He recalls: 'When I started on day one my LinkedIn connections were zero!' He soon realised that most people starting businesses have a bit of heritage behind them that enables them to springboard into what they do. He was conscious that he was behind on the people stakes. 'That was a big problem. I didn't really know anyone so we had to go out and meet all these people; we met them in the incubator.' It was good to take new contacts to a professional space. Charlie was well aware of the challenge ahead. 'We had a small amount of technical ability that came from myself. We had some sales ability but we had to build an incredibly complicated product, a brand-new product from scratch with almost zero financing.'

Accessing funds

Geolise, like most high-tech companies, required a lot of capital. After a couple of years at SETsquared iGeolise were now at a point of getting investment and were pitching to potential investors. This took them overseas where they pitched to US venture capitalists in New York. Charlie concedes: 'We messed up the pitch and so changed our business plan. It's now solid and clear.' Experience is very powerful. They have learnt a lot; it's a question of learning by doing.

According to Charlie, the formula is straightforward. You must decide: How much you need. What you're going to do with it. And what investors will get back. Simple!

They now have a two-stage process, whereby in Stage 1 they must prove their technology commercially and in Stage 2 they will develop new apps. Charlie explains: 'We've got some other investors on board, mainly angel investors.' In addition, they have received some government funding. 'So that's how we finance some of the early stage prototyping.' Research is important and Charlie stresses the importance of knowing your market.

A shift in focus

Originally, iGeolise was going to be a consumer-facing proposition. Charlie explains: 'We wanted to gather users, become a brand name and people would come and search for local content on our site.' However, it was not to prove that simple. 'We quickly realised that to develop the technology, as well as launch a brand name into the consumer market, was going to require millions of pounds.' This was not possible. 'At that stage I was sofa surfing and living out of my car, so I certainly didn't have a million pounds to go and spend on any advertising campaigns!'

They quickly started to think about how they could actually generate income. Charlie was exasperated; he was not simply motivated by money, but keen to actually build something. 'I got quite frustrated with the fact that trying to build a consumer-facing site you could spend an awful lot of time and effort without being able to control the response.' This could be due to a number of reasons. 'It might not have the right market reach that you want.' Unwilling to spend so much resource for very little certainty, they decided to opt for business to business (B2B). Charlie explains: 'B2B allowed us to have a little bit more control and it also meant that we could then reach our first revenue moment faster.' By that he meant: 'The first moment that you ever convince someone to sign on the dotted line and then give you a cheque or cash or a bank transfer.'

They developed their early prototypes to suit their new direction and improved their performance. 'Our algorithms when we first developed them took three to five minutes, now we can do them in 300 milliseconds', Charlie declares. Having focused clearly on the B2B market, they managed to convince their first investor to part with £100,000, 'and we raised that money from a piece of A4 paper and convinced him to have belief in us that we could go and deliver what we were talking about', Charlie says proudly.

Difficult times bring out the best in people; Charlie recalls that this lack of funding 'required us to become quite inventive about how we could get early stage revenues, how we were going to find the right developers, how we were going to pay them and then because we're a B2B, we then have a very long sales pipeline. So it's not as if we can start a consultancy business tomorrow and go out and begin to sell our services. We had a very long wait in which we could actually start selling our first product.' The challenges only grow. 'The problems are infinite and get created more and more every day, but they're good fun and they're quite challenging and that motivates me to do them.'

Since then there have been good days and dark days. 'There have been days when you look at the bank account and it's negative or it's very, very close to zero and you've got bills you need to pay at the end of the month', Charlie recalls with feeling. Despite the tough times, Charlie never wavered in his belief in the business. 'We had developed this technology from the ground up so, it's completely unique.' This, however, had it's own problems. 'There is no other technology at the moment that can do what ours does, so our route to market was quite expensive', Charlie explains. What they did to resolve this was to do some work for their big clients, 'because we had to outlay lots of money before we could get any in we did some work with B2B providing solutions such as: Where should TalkTalk put their new office? Where should the Guardian media group distribute their newspapers to?' These early-stage B2B jobs then enabled them to pump more cash into making the system faster. Their earlier efforts were not wasted as some of the deals that they first tried to secure are coming in to fruition now. 'So now we're seeing growth quite quickly because of all the early leg work that we put in.'

Entrepreneurial skills

'Blind optimism is a pretty good skill or character trait to have', Charlie asserts, thinking about the earlier days. 'I think I've always been quite a personable individual which has helped me do certain things that I might not have been able to do otherwise.' He concedes: 'I am not a very good developer; I'm a very scrappy prototyper. I'm not a very good accountant but I understand accounts. I hate contracts but I have to read them.' It's a process of learning through experience. 'There are lots of skills that I've picked up that enable me to hire the right people for our business. I actually spoke to someone the other day and I just realised my job now is to make my job completely obsolete because there are so many better people than me to go and do all these things.' You need to surround yourself with good people, who are better than you in specialist areas. He is a believer in, 'if you're going to hire someone do their job first'. He says proudly: 'So every single person we've hired in our team I've tried to do some of their job already.' This gives him a deeper insight into all aspects of the business, and yet lets him be free of the minutiae so he can concentrate on the strategy. His most important skill is, 'the whole never giving up, especially on the sales side, and never taking a knock back personally is very, very, very important'.

iGeolise have expanded considerably since the early days and they are now based on City Road, London. The SETsquared model is based on pre-revenue so once a company has reached a certain size they must move on; however, iGeolise still maintain a presence in Guildford and they also have a development office in Kaunas, Lithuania. The company has grown and now has 20 employees.

Many of Charlie's friends have taken the employment route and receive a monthly salary. 'It's really odd as I feel financially stable, which is a thing I haven't really accepted yet.' He left university in debt, like so many students. 'I had to take a Wonga loan out to take my girlfriend on our first date.' He recalls the angst: 'I tried to get jobs at bars, money was a really, really big issue which is why I was sofa surfing, living out of my car, it was pretty hard.' Now, he claims, 'the financial reward is good, not anywhere near to retirement or anything like that but it definitely enables you to remove all of the worry about everything and just not have the desperation that each deal is going to have to mean that you're not going to make rent.'

The next stage

They are now at a stage where, 'we've proven quite heavily in the UK that our technology has a big benefit for our clients and essentially generates them more business as a result, and that's really the stage we wanted to get to because here's a nice product and it looks good, but if it doesn't really do what the client wants, if it essentially doesn't make or save hem money then your product is really dead in the water because people aren't really going to spend any money on it.' They must stay on top of heir game.

The next stage for them is the international market. Charlie says excitedly: 'We're already live in the East and West Coast of America, France, Spain, the Netherlands, Switzerland and Australia and now we're attempting to get more clients in those areas.' They want to repeat the story that they have built up in the UK. Their strategy is to focus on markets that are very similar to the ones they are experienced in such as property, recruitment and tourism. There is scope for growth because the time and distance issue is an international dilemma.

The technology has transformed online searches. Charlie states: 'When you try and search for something online if it tells you it's ten miles away, or it's five miles away, or two and a half miles away you never pick up the phone when you're late and go, I'm two and a half miles away, you say you're 10, 15 minutes away.'

Basically, iGeolise takes the guesswork away from any big decisions by making their location-based searches user-friendly and simple. For example, Charlie elaborates: 'If you are looking for a new home and you get several results from an Internet search, you're having to make lots of effort around whether you would like to live there or if you could get to that job. We remove all of that guess work.' He totally believes in his business. 'It's a valuable technology.'

They want to go beyond just sales. 'What we're also trying to do apart from just sell more product, because that's what helps our business, our investors like it, I like it, my staff like it, is also change the way in which we search for stuff online, and that's the thing we've always wanted to do and make it relevant, much more appealing and much more profitable for businesses.' For a business, that essentially means they can remove location from the question.

iGeolise have a clear strategy for the future: 'We do have many ideas as well, but they all focus around how to make location more relevant.' Charlie explains: 'This idea that if you take a map that was, I can talk to you forever about maps, but maps that were just paper maps, essentially all that's happened is that those maps have been lifted online and then contents have been placed on top of those maps and they are relevant because you know what a map looks like and everyone has a cultural understanding of what a map does. But how many people a day do you see spinning around on a pavement trying to orientate themselves?' He continues: 'We're trying to work on new ways of actually removing location from a question and just driving people to the thing that they actually want.' He is passionate about his business and how it can help people and how it has taken searching to a new level.

Success comes at a big price and now that they are chasing international clients, it means Charlie is travelling a lot: 'I'd love to be able to clone myself in some respects.' He is aware that he has to relinquish control. He says: 'The best way to relinquish control is to give someone that control and then let them make as many mistakes as they can learn incredibly quickly because you can't really breathe down someone's neck on a regular basis; it makes them paranoid. They won't make the decisions you need them to make on their own.' He seems nervous of delegating authority but knows he must.

The past year has meant that Charlie is trying to take a lot of responsibility away from himself, thus enabling him to travel. He has already spent some time in Australia and the US. He feels the weight of having to manage everything back at home as well. 'We need a few more people who would be able to do all the things that I am doing at the moment in the UK, comfortably, safely, as worry-free as possible.' He appreciates how difficult this is. 'I don't think you get to be completely worry-free but it's now the next big thing.'

Looking back at his journey and his success to date, Charlie remains modest: 'There are certain things that have happened that are pure luck.' He explains: 'You meet someone at an event who introduces you to the right person.' However, 'there are other things that take perseverance and time; I don't think there's anything necessarily different about myself; I don't see myself as a big, or different person.' He continues: 'It's just that we came across an idea that worked and we generated a business out of that.' The word entrepreneur is quite an odd thing. 'I think you get called one, you don't necessarily see yourself as one.' He continues: 'I regularly meet people who say "I'm an entrepreneur", and I ask what are you up to? and they say, "I'm in between ideas!"'

Mature for his age, Charlie has had a wealth of experience. 'One of the best things to do with people is just understand their incentives. If you understand someone's incentives you can really work together, whether you're working closely with someone or you're trying to sell to someone.' He is conscious that his partner is of a different age and at a different stage in his life. 'Peter may or may not do something after iGeolise. He has a house, is established, very different from my situation.' Charlie asserts: 'I would like to do lots more things, but the common thing there is we would essentially at some time like a liquidity moment. So we would like to have more than the wage each month as a monetary reward.' Uncertain of the future: 'How that happens I have no idea? There are obviously loads of different ways it could happen; we have no control over those. So with Peter and I it's just about working as we do every day, trying to get as many sales in and grow the business to however large we can and then what we do afterwards, who knows, I'd like to go and sit on a beach for a very long time.'

Charlie's advice to young people is, 'just do it'. He advises them not to overthink. 'I think there's a lot of time to just think and either wind yourself up, drive yourself into a hole, or try and come up with an idea. I think the more you actually do, the more you learn.' He continues: 'You have to find out what you are good at and what you're really bad at because no one's really good at everything but usually someone's at least good at one thing.' He also urges people to think of the bigger picture: 'You need to then understand how that affects other people and what the chain reaction affect is, and you cannot do that in isolation.' You cannot work alone. 'You could be an incredible scientist, you could be the best programmer in the world but unless you can find other people to work with you can't build anything, it's impossible.'

He advises: 'So what you need to do is just get out there and get nervous, get scared, get really fearful.' He recalls: 'When we first started doing public speaking events, or doing sales events, I'd just be freaking out. I used to think I had to wear a suit to everything, so I used to think I had to be somebody else to do the things I wanted to do, because business is all about wearing suits and so on, I don't think I've worn a suit for the past three and a half years, because I was trying to be someone who I wasn't, but I needed to go out and find how I could work with other people and that just meant being myself essentially. But it took a long time and a lot of embarrassing moments and stuff to get there.'

Charlie networked a lot in the early days when he was finding his way around and had more time. 'I think I network quite well with our clients really. We have incredibly good relationships with all our clients.' He continues: 'They can pick up the phone or they'll refer other clients; we hold great responsibility around how we handle our clients.' He understands the importance of maintaining strong relationships, not just for today but to protect them in the future. 'At some point if we keep on doing what we're doing and it goes well we will have competition and at that point there has to be other things that separate you if there's a product that does exactly the same thing.'

He enjoys working with his clients. 'I have a fantastic time, because we work in so many different industries. So I don't just work in recruitment or property, but in lots of sectors, trying to figure out where to put an office location for example.' He thrives on the variety. 'All of those networks in different industries have really exposed me to lots of different things and new ideas. I can be sitting down with the ad agency, a design agency one day about a new application, and the next day I can be trying to map out the Parisian Metro for 2016 as we did for a client the other day.'

So who does Charlie turn to now for advice? 'I have my ultimate sounding board which has always been my dad; he's the biggest sounding board I think for all of his children.' He doesn't have a specific mentor. 'I'm very open to the fact that if I don't understand something or if we screw up, because businesses make mistakes. We have a very honest policy. So if we're in a meeting we don't understand something we just say, do you know what?, I just don't know.'

Charlie has achieved so much, and grown so much in the business but he remains grounded. 'I really don't hold myself in any high regard. I think there's far greater talent and motivation and far more productive individuals than myself. I don't think I will get bored. I think, I've said this a few times, but people are such a big driver for me. I think if I was working in pure isolation I would burn out.' He doesn't think he will be working in maps and location forever, but 'I'll be working with something that people use or that people are involved with', he declares happily.

Summary

Charlie honed in on his love of computers and took time travel to a new dimension enabling people to work with time rather than distance. Hard-working and collaborative, he seeks to understand people and then help them find ways to save or make money. He put in the effort to build up his networks and client base and to gain their trust through strong working relationships based on integrity and sound business practice. Technology businesses require an entrepreneur to keep moving forward at a furious pace; they require a lot of funding and strong business plans to meet the criteria of the investors. Technology businesses can make you a millionaire or more and have global appeal, so start working on your idea.

For more information and to watch an interview with Charlie Davies, please visit our companion website at www.he.palgrave.com/ dhaliwal-millionaire.

Key learnings

- Seek to understand people and then help them
- Build up your networks
- Meet the needs of investors
- Surround yourself with good people
- Delegate authority
- Build customer loyalty
- Never give up.

References

Financial Times (2015). 'Europe's top 50 tech entrepreneurs', 19 June.

Resources

SETsquared Partnership – www.setsquared.co.uk
iGeolise – www.iGeolise.com

11 Entrepreneurial Teams

We talk a lot about the entrepreneur as an individual and many of the discussions and debates surrounding entrepreneurs tend to focus on the individual. In reality, there are many teams that have started a business together and these tend to go on to develop higher value businesses. Kamm *et al.* (1990) define an entrepreneurial team as two or more individuals who jointly establish a business in which they have an equity interest.

Entrepreneurial teams instead of single entrepreneurs start most new high-technology ventures (Lechler, 2001). The reason for this could be that high-tech industries demand more skills of an individual than other industries do. Zhou (2014) also found that shared leadership improves entrepreneurial team performance in his study of technology incubators in China. Investors, too, are keen to understand the team behind the venture before they invest. They want to know about the dynamics of the team, their key skills and their resilience in the face of challenges.

Working in a group enables each member to reflect on their own strengths and weaknesses and build a complementary team. Running a business can be lonely and challenging so to have people who are equally committed and motivated around you can be a real benefit. You can brainstorm together, assess your options and come to a decision – all this has to be based on mutual trust and respect. It's easy for an individual to become overenthusiastic and overoptimistic. A team can have better perspective and it allows others to point out important issues that may have been overlooked by the initiator of the idea.

Working as a team can enable the entrepreneur to do more than they would accomplish alone (Bygrave and Zacharakis, 2014). One consistent finding from both Babson College and London Business School is that businesses with growth aspirations plan on employing more than 20 people within the next five years (Bygrave and Zacharakis, 2014).

Individual entrepreneurs suffer from a limited perspective, little moral support and a small network. Teams have a better chance of success due to an increased skill set, an improved capacity for innovation and a higher social level of support among other factors (Bygrave and Zacharakis, 2014). Most new ventures suffer from more pitfalls than milestones at the launch phase so resilience is essential and having shared responsibility to work hard, as well as moral support and the sharing of confidential problems, can prevent the business from folding.

Business is all about relationships – be they with suppliers, customers or investors. Well-networked individuals make better entrepreneurs but a team dramatically multiplies the size of even a good network. Build your team wisely. A team is also better for investors who want a return on their capital and a team is better placed for this than relying on one individual.

Of course, teams can also have conflicts and challenges of their own, but in the high-tech world they are essential. The following case illustrates the strengths of a team.

Conno Christou – Avocarrot

Conno Christou boasts the kind of life many high-tech wannabees only dream of. His eventful business life, which started at the age of 24, has taken him from Cyprus and London to the US Silicon Valley and Athens. He is part of a strong team initiated by four friends and culminating in their company Avocarrot, a network site for native advertising. Avocarrot has also been recognised as one of the eight best companies by Google for Entrepreneurs in a global competition and voted as the 'Next Big Thing' at the advertising technology conference ad:tech in 2013. They are set to take the world by storm.

Conno is a Greek-Cypriot who grew up in Cyprus in a creative family. His father is an artist and his mother is a physiotherapist. He has a brother who is an artist and director and a sister who is a cellist, both are younger than him.

Conno met George Eracleous, George Makkoulis and Panos Papageorgiou when they were on military service in Cyprus. All males born to a Cypriot or Greek-Cypriot parents are obliged to do 24 months' service in the military. They bonded over the two years, little knowing then how fortuitous their meeting was. The four friends later studied together at

Imperial College, London; their subject choices varied but were mainly in the fields of Computer Science and Electrical Engineering.

In 2012 when Conno was 24 years old, they started a business together, initially for fun, and to their surprise won first prize for a fashion app called Fasham at the London Hackathon. This is where developers and engineers descend from all over the world to take part in a 24-hour hacking endurance test. Teams join forces to build a new product, present it on stage to a panel of expert judges and an audience of tens of thousands and compete for a variety of prizes.

Having won first prize, they were euphoric. The user engagement rate was very high and their app was well liked so they got together and thought, 'how do we make money from this?' They knew they were on to something big.

They set themselves the task of going forward and making money from their creation. They tried banners but these didn't work. Banners are a heading or advertisement appearing on a web page in the form of a bar, column or box. 'Users didn't click on them as they were outside the user's experience and a distraction to users', Conno explains. Thus they did not get enough clicks or make any money. This proved very frustrating for the group.

Determined to succeed and still full of self-confidence they persevered and started writing their own ad technology, which later on was formalised into a legal entity, called 'Avocarrot', complete with a logo and the strapline: 'Beautiful native ads that match the look & feel of any app. Monetize smart and keep your users happy' (Avocarrot.com).

They had found a way to embed the apps that was integrated, targeted and relevant and found they got a lot more clicks and revenue was increased. There was a higher rate of return for investors so it was a win-win situation, with all parties making money. The team soon stopped producing apps and focused on this 'native' advertising.

The simplest way to define native ads is to say they are advertisements that don't look like advertisements. Instead they adopt the shape and form of 'native' content for the platform on which they appear, blending in seamlessly and bypassing consumers' resistance towards commercial messages. In this way, the recipients can consume the message alongside normal content without clumsy interruption of their natural mental flow (Avocarrot.com).

Native ads work far better than banner ads or interstitials, with around 70 per cent of customers preferring this method to traditional advertising.

this may be true to an even greater extent in the context of mobile advertising, where users have very little patience for aggressive product pushing. The human mind erects barriers to protect itself against information overload and less invasive ads are more likely to slip through the cracks. Furthermore, many users feel like native promos have real information value and are often ready to share them with others without any external motivation (Avocarrot.com).

They were on to a winner. But they needed finance.

They went to Entrepreneur First, which is Europe's leading pre-seed investment programme for technical founders (www.joinef.com). Conno recalls: 'Going to Entrepreneur First, which is an accelerator, was the greatest thing we could have done back then.' They needed to get a good grasp of a technical business. Basic concepts are important for high-growth technology companies, which can go global. Entrepreneur First was well placed to mentor and educate them to achieve their ambitions.

Entrepreneur First was a very important step for the team. They had a good idea that was working, but to get up to speed and compete in a global setting the boys knew they needed help. They needed so much at that point and Entrepreneur First offered intensive mentoring and education, filling many of the gaps they had in terms of business so they learnt a lot about writing a business plan, executing a business, all the financial aspects, as well as pitching, marketing and so on.

They also got funding from Collider12. Collider is an accelerator dedicated to marketing and advertising start-ups. Collider 'inject smart capital, expert coaching and forge commercial connections' (www.collider.io). They received £100,000 from Collider; the money in the Collider fund was provided by investors, including Unilever, Bauer Media, Ingenious Media and other angels with advertising expertise.

The transformational point was in about July 2013 when Google selected them as one of the best companies with potential. Avocarrot was selected from a strong field of thousands of high-tech companies. The team was taken to Silicon Valley in San Francisco where they attended a three-week immersion programme. The team met very impressive people, such as the founders of Twitter and YouTube. This really was a global platform of the highest degree. Conno recalls: 'What really impressed me was how humble these people were. Many of them were billionaires, had global outreach yet would come to work in T-shirts jeans and on bicycles or in modest cars. It was so far fetched from the shallowness of Los

Angeles, for example.' These were values Conno respected. People here loved what they did and would work hard to ensure they got the best out of themselves.

They went on to win another prize from ad:tech, a global conference for advertising technology. Conno recalls proudly: 'We were voted as The Next Big Thing at ad:tech London in September 2013 from a panel of investors and advertising experts.' Ad-tech London is where the UK's marketing and media players meet for technology discovery, cutting-edge content and unrivalled networking (www.ad-techlondon.co.uk). They were selected out of 100 companies – ten judges, who were also investors, selected Avocarrot and there was a huge press and media interest in them. This led to a move to San Francisco where they managed to get investment of half a million US dollars from Silicon Valley and another 2 million dollars from various angels and investors in the US. Their success was solid.

This was a whirlwind journey for Conno. At the beginning, Conno recalls: 'I was overconfident. If I knew what the next three years would be like, how scary it could be I would have felt differently.' Ignorance is bliss it seems.

He looks back at his short journey: 'Going to Silicon Valley was a massive jump professionally and personally.' He credits the strong team of four as essential to the success of Avocarrot. 'To have four like-minded people getting the best out of each other and being committed is amazing', he declares.

Conno's advice to others is to find the right team. 'The single most important ingredient for success is finding the right people to work with. Ideas come and go; you can generate many ideas, some of them will work, many just simply won't. It's the execution that's important. You need to work with people who have integrity, trust, commitment and work hard and really push each other to get the best out of themselves and each other.' He continues: 'There are so many challenges businesses face, so many problems and really much of the time you don't know how to deal with them. You must be in a supportive environment with people you trust and have the know-how and the acumen to go forward.'

Conno credits each of the founders as exceptional in terms of their work ethic and they are 'super productive and focused'. He asserts that they 'complement each other'. The right team is the catalyst to success it is the single most important ingredient to success.

Conno's family are important to him. 'I am extremely lucky that both my parents are open-minded and trust me fully on my personal and career endeavours. This means that it's been a good three years that they don't completely understand the whats/hows/whens? of what we actually do and try to envision but they are definitely proud parents for seeing their children being happy with what they do.'

Conno had dabbled with the idea of entrepreneurship as a possible future route when he was growing up, but not too seriously. ' I tried a few things such as hobby or lifestyle businesses', but, he confesses, 'I've always been into geeky stuff'. He really had no idea that he would be an entrepreneur with his friends. 'Our University education was to take us into banking or consultancy', he asserts, but the four friends resisted. They set their sights on bigger things.

Conno is a realist. 'Entrepreneurship is not for everyone. Starting up a business is not for everyone; it's for people who can be psychologically strong.' By that he means: 'They have to manage their psychology; there are so many challenges along the way, a lot of lows, a lot of worries; you must be strong; you must be resilient. The founder especially has a difficult job.'

Conno reflects on his strengths: 'I am curious. I am curious about life, about business about everything and that's what drives me.' He also states: 'I am confident, not arrogant. Confidence is essential, people buy people, they need that confidence, and they need to believe in them. They need that assurance and therefore you have to be confident; you've got to be confident about yourself as well as your business.'

Work ethic is important. 'You must be 100 per cent committed, you have to be ready to make compromises at times. There is no personal life; you have to make sacrifices, big compromises.'

It is easy to understand why Conno is at the helm of a global business. 'To get exceptional output, exceptional input is needed. You have to play your 'A' game all the time, you have to be focused, committed and ready and willing at all times.'

He continues: 'You cannot copy others; success cannot be replicated. You have to learn by doing. You have to fail many, many times; the failure rate is very high for most successful people.' Conno confesses that sometimes he lacks focus: ' I must prioritise my time. Time is money.'

A bigger team has joined the original four co-founders. Today, there are 15 people in the company and it's growing. They have opened new offices in Athens and they still maintain a presence in San Francisco.

Summary

Conno and his co-founders have certainly built up a good relationship and a good business. They exemplify the strengths of teamwork and have been successful in taking their business to a global level. They are not afraid to enter competitions, admit they need help and then to take all the advice on board. They have a truly global offering in an intensely competitive field, but it is their love of work and being exceptional with their business that keeps them going rather than the shallow trimmings of success. They are young entrepreneurs to watch in the future.

Key learnings

- Find the right people to work with – get the right team
- Enter competitions and win
- Develop a winning pitch
- Prioritise your time
- Develop strong networks and relationships
- Confidence is essential; arrogance is not
- Think global
- Always play your 'A' game.

References

Bygrave, W. D. and A. Zacharakis, A. (2014). *Entrepreneurship*, 3rd edition, Wiley.

Kamm, J. B., J. C. Shuman, J. A. Seeger and A. J. Nurick (1990). 'Entrepreneurial teams in new venture creation: a research agenda', *Entrepreneurship: Theory and Practice*, vol. 14, no. 4, pp. 7–17.

Kamm, J. B. and A. J. Nurick (1993). 'The stages of team venture formation: a decision-making model', *Entrepreneurship: Theory and Practice*, vol. 17, no. 2, pp. 17–27.

Lechler, T. (2001). 'Social interaction: a determinant of entrepreneurial team venture success', *Small Business Economics*, vol. 16 no. 4, pp. 263–78.

Wencang Z. (2014). 'When does shared leadership matter in entrepreneurial teams: the role of personality composition?', International *Entrepreneurship and Management Journal*, vol. 12, no. 1, pp. 1–17.
http://link.springer.com/article/10.1007%2Fs11365-014-0334-3, date accessed 13 July 2014.

Resources

Avocarrot – www.avocarrot.com
Entrepreneur First – www.joinef.com

# 12 Job Creation

The island of Barbados in the Caribbean is a haven for the rest of the world desperate for some sunshine. Canadians, Europeans and Americans flock to the island, which boasts the finest beaches, rum and music in the world.

I'm sitting on a lounger watching the waves lap the shore with the beat of the music in the background. I see a few clouds but it's hot; the sea is turquoise and varying shades of blue with the froth of the waves as they come into shore. I see some swimmers at a distance bobbing in the water. A jet ski goes by and then a catamaran and a speedboat. It's a good day. No cruise ships today; the island is peaceful.

Barbados has much to boast about. The capital, Bridgetown, has a harbour, restaurants and many, many taxi drivers touting for business. Tourists flock to the department store Cave Shepherd for their hexagon-shaped coconut cakes and rum. A quick tour around the Bacardi factory, a visit to Oistins, the fish market, on a Friday night and a trip to windy Bathsheba, a surfer's paradise, are a must. Barbados is an island for people with depth and soul. Rihanna may not be the biggest export in Barbados – cricket, tourists and sugar play a big role.

The main industries in Barbados are tourism and international financial services. In terms of exports, tourism is considered an invisible export as it earns foreign exchange, while visible exports are sugar, rum and light manufacturing, mainly food and beverage.

Despite the beauty of the island and its natural resources and climate the Caribbean has a serious youth unemployment problem. Not only is youth unemployment high, relative to global levels, it is also significantly higher than adult unemployment. The average youth unemployment rate for countries in the region with available data was nearly 25 per cent in 2013, compared with the adult rate of only 8 per cent (Lashley et al., 2015).

According to Warren Smith, President of the Caribbean Development Bank: 'High levels of youth unemployment inhibit economic development ... It is a critical development concern that requires urgent attention and durable solutions' (Lashley *et al.,* 2015, p. 6). The report suggests priority objectives which include skills for employment and entrepreneurship as well as creating decent jobs, social protection and the promotion of active participation in the labour market. It is proposed that compulsory training in entrepreneurial skills such as leadership, business financial skills and business management would not only assist in the creation of an entrepreneurial class, it would also make for better employees, as it would provide an appreciation of how businesses operate, and has the potential to drive internal innovation (intrapreneurship).

Young entrepreneurs are also more likely to hire other young people. They are responsive to new economic opportunities and trends, and young people with entrepreneurial skills make better employees (Kew *et al.,* 2013). Entrepreneurship offers unemployed and discouraged youth a way forward to develop new skills and these can be applied to other challenges in life. Below we look at one young entrepreneur who has risen to the challenge.

I'm at the beach in Rockley, Christchurch, Barbados, to meet Corey Boyce, owner of Supreme Delight.

Corey Anderson Boyce – Supreme Delight

Barbados-born and bred, Corey Anderson Boyce is a young man with a mission. He wants to be employed and to provide employment to as many others as he can. Frustrated with being out of work or in low-paid seasonal work, Corey decided to take his destiny into his own hands in his mid-twenties and to create a business from the best the island has to offer. Sweet-toothed, Corey is the owner of the fledgling company Supreme Delights, bringing traditional confectioneries with an added twist with the different flavours. He is trying to cater for the old and the new. Older Bajans (Barbadians) tend to have a sweet tooth and like the traditional flavours, but many young people are unaware of these items – thus traditional flavours for the old, and non-traditional for the new.

Shy, reticent Corey Anderson Boyce always shunned the limelight as a student. He was thoughtful, hard-working and respectful of those around him. Corey has two younger brothers and a sister and, as the oldest, he has the pressure of being their role model. Corey had a challenging time growing up; he was bullied at school because he was small. He had to focus a lot of time and energy dealing with negative peer pressure and trying to turn it into a strength. This difficult childhood opened his eyes and he did his best to turn this weakness into a strength.

After going through his primary, secondary and tertiary education he completed an Associate degree in Culinary Arts at the Barbados Hospitality Institute. Eager to find work and put his education to the test, Corey found it hard going in the working world. In the workplace he was turned down for many jobs. He applied for several others but was constantly turned down. This proved frustrating. In addition, any hotel work he did get was seasonal.

Some years he managed to some seasonal work in the hotels but he was often unemployed for periods at a time. This did not sit well with the hard-working family-oriented young man. He found himself looking for jobs on a regular basis, and even while in work he did not feel secure, knowing his contracts would soon end. This was no way to build a future and make the most of his talents and abilities.

On occasion, entrepreneurship can be a matter of necessity rather than desire. The economy took a turn for the worse and Corey's mother was also unemployed. Corey was therefore determined to get out of the hole they were in. He found it futile facing no future. He had to take control. He also wanted to help others.

It was when Corey was made unemployed again after a particularly good spell in a hotel that he realised he had to take matters into his own hands. He was just 25, with three young siblings and was the man of the house. He had to do something. He was no longer prepared to put up with being unemployed.

'It got so bad', he recalls, and when he was laid off again from a hotel during the low season, he thought: 'I can't keep going on like this.' He listed his talents and realised he liked cooking. 'I was going to buy a van and do some cooking and sell it in the streets.'

Knowing what you don't know is an important part of entrepreneurship. Corey was astute, and turned to organisations in Barbados for some help. At this time he took advice from a Barbados Youth Business Trust and the Youth Entrepreneurship Scheme (YES). He called YES first and talked through his idea with one of the consultants. The advice he was given was not to buy a van. This would be too expensive to get a loan to start up. Instead, the consultant, who then became his mentor, suggested the confectionery business after talking through his talents, experiences and abilities.

Corey was fired up. He was motivated to start his own business; he just needed an open door and an opportunity and this consultant had given him one. Corey went home and started researching the idea immediately. He wanted to add a twist to original confectionery. Using local produce he makes rum and raisin sugar cakes, berries and cherries as well as sorrel sugar cake. He wanted to resurrect a dying art, as today not many people go to the trouble of making tamarind balls or sugar cakes.

From an idea the business turned into a mission. Young people like Corey had lost the art of confectionery-making, the tradition was lost. He decided to start making traditional Bajan confectionery and utilise local crops, including sweet potato, yams and cassava to make 'snack chips'. Corey is keen to use local produce; he is proud of his Bajan roots and the richness that the island has to offer. He uses only fresh, local ingredients – no preservatives. Natural produce such as sugar cane, which Barbados boasts in abundance, coconut, spices and yams are all used in his sugar cakes. His chips are made from sweet potato, yams and breadfruit.

This was a promising start with the youth entrepreneurship scheme and he continued his conversation with his mentor. He conducted his market research and realised that he had established competitors, so he added a twist to his sugar cakes using different shapes and flavours. He even got an award as the most outstanding participant with YES.

He launched his business in 2014 at the Barbados Manufacturers Export Exhibition (BMEX) and came in second in the new product show-case competition.

Risk-averse Corey took out no loan initially; he started small. No capital. Just ten Barbados dollars to his name and from this he purchased sugar, coconut and the other ingredients to bake his first batch of sugar cakes. He sold these and re-invested the profits and so has grown gradually and safely.

Corey understood that he needed training and so from March to November of 2014 he learnt about market research, business planning, structuring your business and the different components of the business. His hard work paid off and at the end of the year he won Entrepreneur of the Year Award 2014.

Still, with a young company barely off the ground, Corey recalls the challenges he faced: 'I was alone, untrained with no money.' His sugar cakes sold for just two Barbados dollars so his income was low. He lacked knowledge and business record-keeping. The competition was strong and established. Finance was difficult.

He eventually got a small grant from YES for a sealer to seal his cakes; he also bought labels and T-shirts. The Youth Business Trust (YBT) also offered assistance. They provided training, sales and marketing opportunities, a grant, and Corey at the time of writing had just approached them for a loan. He also attended BMEX workshops and soon built a name and a reputation and, despite being so shy, he received a lot of media attention

To overcome some of the challenges he faced, his mother, Joanna Boyce, became a key part of the business. She produces the goods and Corey concentrates on sales and marketing. A neighbour, Anita Francis handles the packaging, product development and administration. Thus it is a tight-knit operation. They work from home and so that reduces costs still further although Corey is keen to move into larger premises as his customer base expands.

His customer base includes tourist offices, locals, as well as events and weddings. The popular months are October to December where sales are high. Independence day is an important calendar event that is celebrated and Christmas is popular. The Marriott Hotel stocks his products and even the president of Venezuela loved his sugar cakes. His clientele is growing.

Corey wants eventually to ship overseas but the drawback is that his products contain no preservatives and so have a short shelf life. He still needs to think this through. He wants to build up the business a little more and then maybe build plants in other countries so his products can stay fresh and retain their authenticity. At the moment interest in him and his products is high.

Having won Entrepreneur of the Year in 2014 and been feted by the media and locals alike, Corey remains shy and grounded. 'I don't like the exposure', he admits but realises the benefits of it to his business.

He has met others along the way who have started a business but they gave up when the going got tough. 'It's not easy running a business here', says Corey, referring to the high levels of unemployment on the island, particularly for young people. He faced insecurity and uncertainty. He did not have the funds or money. However, he was determined. 'Failure is not an option for me', he asserts. 'I don't give up.'

Many of his peers have given up – it takes grit and determination to keep going but Corey won't settle for a wasted life. In total, to date, he has won Entrepreneur of the Year 2014, two silver medals and one bronze from the National Independence Festival of Creative Arts (NIFCA) culinary competition.

His advice to others is real; he pulls no punches: 'Quite honestly it is a hard journey.' He advises young people to 'focus on where you want to be'. After all, 'you will face a lot of challenges but focus on where you want to go. Family and friends will pull you down'. You must 'carry on, and work hard; stay focused'. Find something unique or add a twist to something that works. As Corey says, 'don't reinvent the wheel', but be creative.

His aspirations are to have premises – to be bigger than Pringles. 'I want to be comfortable.' He is inspired by people enjoying his products. He loves seeing people's faces when they taste his sweets – the joy. It overcomes his shyness.

Corey has managed to turn a hobby into a business and has taken a mature risk-averse approach: 'Not too fast, not too soon.' Therefore he purposefully didn't take out a loan at the beginning of his venture, as he wanted to gain knowledge first. He knew what he wanted.

Corey is working hard to professionalise his business with the limited capital he has, relying on his own resources where possible. He is on Facebook and Instagram and busily building his website. I see him in action as he tries to pitch to the hotel I am staying at. He lets them sample his products in his subtle yet confident style and is met with respect and asked to email them his price list. Another success.

When I finish my interview with Corey, I go back to the beach and watch the waves pounding, froth at the tips. I go for a swim. Standing at the edge of the water I am pounded by the waves; they crash into me, knocking me off balance. As I looked further out to sea, I saw people calmly swimming, bobbing and jumping the waves.

Perhaps entrepreneurship is like these waves: rough at the edges looking in but smoother with a few bumps from within.

Summary

Proud of his Bajan roots and with clear family values, Corey set out on a mission to help others escape unemployment. Motivated by his own desire to escape the insecurity of seasonal contracts followed by periods of unemployment, he decided to set up his own business. He appreciated his knowledge gaps and was keen to ask for help and listen to advice, while taking control of the business decisions himself. He turned to organisations on the island for help, and this was provided in terms of advice, mentorship and enhanced publicity as well as some financial help. Corey was wise not to take on debt, and worked hard using his own labour and that of family and friends. His mission is still clear and he wants to grow and provide jobs for others. After winning Entrepreneur of the Year, and being recognised by the press and the industry, he is set to fulfil his dreams.

Key learnings

- Make a decision to start a business and then be single-minded
- Know what you don't know and seek help
- Put a twist on a traditional business
- Take care when and on what you invest your money
- Surround yourself with people you trust
- Push yourself out of your comfort zone and sell
- Develop a media profile; its good for business
- Enter competitions and aspire to be the best you can be!

References

Cumberbatch, Shawn (2014). 'Snackers' delight', *Nation News*, 13 July, http://www.nationnews.com/nationnews/news/55417/snackers-delight#sthash.tu3VyG8E.dpuf, date accessed 4 November 2015.

Kew, J., M. Herrington, Y. Litovsky and H. Gale (2013). *Generation Entrepreneur? The state of global youth entrepreneurship.* Joint Report: Global Enterprise Monitor (GEM) and Youth Business International (YBI).

Lashley, J., D. Marshall, C. Bailey, C. Crawford, L. Lazarus and K. Lord. (2015). *The youth are the future: the imperative of youth employment for sustainable development in the Caribbean.* Caribbean Development Bank. http://www.caribank.org/wp-content/uploads/2016/05/Study_Micro-Small-and-Medium-Enterprise-Development.pdf, date accessed 5 September 2015.

Conclusion

Every one of these young entrepreneurs is a real person, a well-rounded character, with all the traits that real people have. All are driven. Some work through conviction and others through consensus. All of them are achievers, all of them are interesting, and all of them have a story worth reading. These people are real and they are inspiring.

Georgie Bullen has the same energy, drive and self-confidence in her business that won her a place in the Paralympics. Her Goalball business was launched with her Paralympian credentials as the unique selling point, and she won't take no for an answer as she seeks any opportunity to pitch her business.

Amit Pate was determined to come to the UK and pursue his high-tech anti-counterfeiting business idea. He was inspired by events around him and really listened to the market, changing course when he realised he was out of his depth. Solveiga Pakštaitė demonstrated curiosity, courage and determination in her fight to find a solution to food waste. She was like a detective until she found the solution with her Bump Mark technology and had an extraordinary journey along the way. Charlie Davies was prepared to work in his parents' loft until he found premises for his high-tech, innovative company iGeolise, which looks at time rather than distance and has made an enormous impact already. These young entrepreneurs will stop at nothing to succeed and show tremendous amounts of courage, conviction and a strong work ethic.

The world has changed so much. It is a riskier place and a more uncertain place. Jobs seem to be difficult to find and even harder to keep. There is no safe job for life any more and young people need to behave in entrepreneurial ways. You need to be alert to opportunities, agile and skilled. You need to think bigger.

It's an exciting world too. Now more than ever before it is possible to set up a business quickly and cheaply. The reality is, however, that to sustain and grow this business you need to have thought it through, accessed help and advice, got yourself a mentor and sourced finance.

There are some fascinating graduate businesses. Nigel Westwood put a new spin on a traditional business with his innovative furniture designs, while Kristian Else gave a voice to people who really needed one and turned his social endeavour into a business while helping overseas students with their accommodation woes.

Money and mentors come hand in hand and both are crucial. Young entrepreneurs need support. Running a business can be challenging, lonely and downright frightening so you need to surround yourself with good people or, better still, work in a team as Conno Christou did with his company Avocarrot, and he has gone on to experience global success with his co-founders.

We've established we need young entrepreneurs. They will bring fresh impetus to the economy. We need leaders, calculated risk-takers and go-getters. Young entrepreneurs are the new entrepreneurial heroes required to save the world. Governments are also doing much to motivate and inspire entrepreneurs through their various initiatives, and accelerators are proving a useful mechanism for many high-growth, high-tech businesses. Matthew Simmonds and his team turned to accelerator Entrepreneur First to stay ahead of the game, and honed in on a gap in the market for the elderly with their SpeakSet business idea. Other organisations such as The Prince's Trust have done much to promote an entrepreneurial culture for the young and boast many success stories, including Demi Owoseje and Gabrielle Evans who both turned to enterprise whilst unemployed. Corey decided to take matters into his own hands when the Barbados-based young man was made unemployed again for the umpteenth time.

Young entrepreneurs are astute at spotting opportunities. Many have had the seeds of enterprise sewn while they were at university. Academic institutions can do much to promote this. After all, an enterprising graduate will always be employable. Sarah Yull is inspirational in that she went to university with a business idea and then used her degree to enhance her profits. She went to study with a clear purpose and so he university degree was rewarding both for her and her Yull shoe business. Both grew during this period.

Your time at university is a great opportunity to experiment. If universities are safe places to fail, then this is a chance to be a risk-taker and learn from the experience.

Enterprise should be a part of the curriculum for schools, colleges and universities. We have an enterprise week in the UK which runs in November each year and this enables students and others to showcase their talents in all sorts of ways. Many schools now embrace entrepreneurship and children get into groups to develop ideas and then sell, sell, sell. Enterprise societies at colleges and universities have gained momentum and are starting to produce some serious businesses.

Few start-ups are created straight after graduation. Normally students work for a few years and then they become frustrated and start up on their own. Perhaps today's graduates are not hungry enough? Or frustrated enough? 'The role of entrepreneurship education may be to sow the seeds that emerge later, setting people up for future success so they know what opportunities look like and can grab them', according to Dave Jarman, Bath Spa University. Entrepreneurship is an ability to navigate the complex situations, to spot opportunities and to grab opportunities.

Young entrepreneurs create jobs for other young people. The team around the founder of a new firm plays a crucial role in the development and success of the company and may go on to start their own ventures. Young people are more likely to employ other young people thus helping youth unemployment. Young people must make things happen, not wait for them. They must create opportunities, not wait for an opportunity to open up for them.

The young entrepreneurs featured in this book didn't just dream about starting a business, they went for it. Many started small. They made mistakes, they lost money, they felt insecure but they grew from their experience. They surrounded themselves with strong networks, good mentors and put in the time and effort to learn. They all work hard – some of them in traditional business; many of them in high-tech businesses. They work long hours and are committed and mature for their age. They're having fun building up businesses that make a difference and that they can be proud of. Their futures are more promising as a result.

So, if you're still thinking about starting your own business – go on, give it a try!

References

Jarman, D. (2014). *Encouraging student and graduate entrepreneurship – support and finance for start-ups, and implementing the Enterprise Education Review.* Westminster Higher Education Forum Keynote Seminar, 9 December.

Index